LEADERS

OF OUR
PEOPLE

BOOK II

LEADERS OF OUR PEOPLE

BOOK II

RABBI JOSEPH H. GUMBINER

Illustrated by David Stone

Union of American Hebrew
Congregations • New York

EDITOR'S INTRODUCTION

WE ARE DELIGHTED TO OFFER THIS SECOND VOLUME OF JOSEPH H. Gumbiner's biographical sketches to our readers. First published in an experimental edition, his work found sufficiently wide acceptance to warrant its reproduction in this more permanent form. Rabbi Gumbiner writes well, and his words reflect his great love for our people and the depth of his faith.

Some stories included in the experimental volume were deleted; new biographies were added; and the entire work was carefully re-written. The process of revision was supervised by Mrs. Rayanna Simons of the Union's educational staff and much of the editorial credit must go to her. The book's over-all design reflects the considerable skill and care of our Production Manager, Mr. Ralph Davis.

We also wish to acknowledge the contribution of Mrs. Rebecca Lister, a reader for the Commission on Jewish Education, who perused the original manuscript and made many valuable suggestions for its improvement.

We tell these stories to our children to give them knowledge concerning the lives of our great men in the hope that this knowledge will secure their self-acceptance, that it will nourish their determination to be Jews, and that—above all—it will awaken their awareness of the God Who shapes the destiny of Israel.

RABBI ALEXANDER M. SCHINDLER
Director of Education

CONTENTS

LEADERS

OF OUR
PEOPLE

BOOK II

1

LUIS DE TORRES
Into the Uncharted Sea

SEPTEMBER 30, 1492

Aboard the SANTA MARIA

IT IS almost impossible to write; the Santa Maria pitches and rolls in these stormy seas and the candles flicker uneasily, but I must record this while it is fresh in my mind. I have decided that our leader ("Admiral of the Ocean Sea" is what he likes to be called) is either the world's greatest, bravest explorer—or insane!

On deck this morning, the terrified sailors huddled together, whispering. I know they were ready to mutiny. Small wonder! It has been three weeks since we left the last island

3

off the coast of Africa behind us (it was the 9th of September) and headed steadily west, out into the open, uncharted sea.

Is Colon afraid, too? Does he ever wonder how we shall be able to sail back to Spain, when the wind blows always from the east, pushing us further and further into the great, grey sea, and always westward?

If he is afraid, he shows no trace of it. When he faced the angry, frightened crew this morning, his voice was strong and confident, and there was no fear on his bronzed face.

"Stop being fools and cowards," he told the men. "We are going to the Indies, and we sail westward to reach the Far East. We shall reach our destination and you will all be rich beyond your wildest dreams!" His eyes blazed with excitement. "Courage! *Adelante! Adelante!* Sail on! Sail on!"

When he had finished, the sailors became calm and returned quietly to their posts.

But I—I am not a simple man of the sea to be so easily reassured. I, Luis de Torres, master of Arabic, Hebrew and Aramaic, interpreter to the Admiral, why did *I* become party to this foolish, wild adventure? Why am I caged in this close, ill-smelling cabin, living on mouldy hardtack and dried beef that looks and tastes like ancient leather?

I know that no one will read this diary, surely not while I am alive. Therefore I may allow myself the pleasure of being honest, at least privately.

I am here I suppose, because, like some of the others, I am a Jew, so deeply in my heart that I cannot and will not change. Their Catholic Majesties gave me a choice which was no choice at all. "Convert," they said, "become a Christian—or go into exile."

4

Exile! I would have gone gladly, leaving the beloved sun-warmed mountains and valleys of Spain forever without a backward glance, had I not known there was no place to go. Not one in ten of those Jews who chose exile will live to set foot in a new land, or find a new home.

A few days before we sailed, another ship of Jews was leaving the harbor. They had chosen exile rather than conversion.

Poor souls! Many others have sailed—their ships were sunk, they were set upon by pirates, and for those who survived the perilous voyages, the countries from which they expected haven turned them away.

So—I was baptized with so many others and became a secret Jew, pretending to accept the Christian religion, but practicing my true faith stealthily, in secret. The Spaniards call us "Marranos"—an old Spanish word which means, simply, "swine." It is a name we accept, and not without pride.

We are hated—homeless—masqueraders. But if the Admiral is correct and we do find the short route to the Indies, perhaps we Jews may yet find a new home. Perhaps there are islands, far-off places where we will be welcome, where we will not be forced to pretend to be what we can never be.

OCTOBER 2, 1492

For two days the winds have steadied, and I have had time to think. There is something very mysterious about this

5

voyage and the people who made it possible. Who, for example, put up the money for these ships and for the crews? Everyone knows it was Luis de Santangel and Gabriel Sanchez, treasurers to King Ferdinand and Queen Isabella. Both of these men are "Christians," "New Christians," but I know they are Marrano Jews, just as I am. (Is this why young Rodrigo Sanchez is on this voyage—to make sure that the money his family raised is spent for the proper purpose?)

Could the Admiral have possibly left Palos without the precious maps made by Yehudah Cresques and Abraham Zacuto? The astronomer Zacuto also supplied the astrolabe. Without it we could not chart our course through this great ocean. Both these men are Marranos. I know.

When the sailors fall sick, who cares for them? It is the ship's physician, our own Maestro Bernal. He is here for the same reason that I, Luis de Torres, am here, and Sanchez too. It is because we wish again to pray to one God without the terror of the Inquisition always upon us—to find a land of peace and freedom. May God help us find even a speck of land beyond this rolling, endless sea!

What of the Admiral himself, Cristobal Colon? Why is *he* here? Yes, of course he wishes to reach the wealth of the Indies of which so many have dreamed. But does that explain this insane expedition? Is there no other way to gold and fame for him but this perilous journey, on and on into the uncharted, unknown sea?

I have had much time to observe the Admiral and I have noticed some strange things about him. They say he comes from Genoa, in Italy. But I am a student of languages, many languages, and it is clear to me that the man knows no

Italian whatsoever! He speaks only Spanish, and when he tries to write in Latin he writes Latin of a kind that a Spanish-speaking man would write. I cannot unravel this mystery—unless what some have dared to whisper is true!

Colon never speaks of his family. But I know that he has many friends among Marranos. It is said that he is much interested in the history of the Jews. I am told that he reckons dates by our ancient Hebrew calendar, and that he calls Jerusalem the "navel of the world."

Then too—what's in a name? But some Marranos are known by the name Colon. It is rumored that to his son, Diego, he has repeatedly said that the name must never be altered, even slightly, even to "Colum," or any other spelling.

There are rumors, too, that in his messages to his son, the pages bear two letters which look like the second and fifth letters of our Hebrew alphabet—a *bes* and a *heh*, like this: ב and ה. I note this for a reason. In the days when Jews wrote freely to each other, without fear of being known as Jews, these letters were used as a kind of greeting. They stood for *b'ezras ha Shem*, "with the help of God!" Is it possible that the Admiral really uses this sign? And if he does can he know its meaning?

And there is one thing more which I cannot forget. On August 2nd, we were completely prepared to sail out of the harbor at Palos. Provisions were on board, the ship was in readiness, the sailors stood at their stations waiting for the signal to weigh anchor, and the wind was with us. Why did Colon wait until a half-hour before sunrise of the next day, August 3rd? Was this because he knew, as I do, that August

7

2nd of this year was the 9th day of Ov in our Hebrew calendar, the day which our tradition has marked as the fearful day that the First and the Second of our ancient Temples were destroyed? Or was this coincidence? Did the Admiral share our superstition that ventures begun on Tisho B'ov end in disaster?

These are puzzles I cannot answer. Nor do I wish to know the answers. In such times as these, it is not safe to know too much of any man's secrets.

OCTOBER 12, 1492

Darkness had fallen when I returned to the ship tonight. It may be that I am the first white man ever to have set foot upon that strange shore. In the shadows, Colon waited for me on the lower deck. "Come quickly," he said. "It is very late. I have waited for your return in a fever of impatience. We shall eat while you tell me what you have seen."

I was exhausted from the tropical sun and from the excitement of what I had discovered, but I could eat nothing and I could not stop talking. The words poured from me in torrents. The Admiral's eyes never left my face, nor did he interrupt me.

"It is amazing!" I said. "It is as though we had landed on another planet! This is indeed a new world, utterly new! Not a single animal . . . not a single bird have I seen or heard of before such as these! How did these living creatures and the men I found come to this far-away place? Did men of long

It may be that I am the first white man ever to have set foot upon that strange shore.

ago once walk over all the earth before the deep waters divided it?"

The Admiral leaned forward. "What language do these people speak?"

"None that I have ever heard before, my Admiral. It is unlike any language known to us . . . even the most ancient . . . Greek, Latin, Hebrew, Arabic, Aramaic. Nor do I think it resembles any language of the Orient.

"The men I found say that their forbears came from the north. This made me think of the hardy Norsemen who sailed thousands of miles over water in their tiny boats, from island to island. But I do not think their ancestors were Norse. There is nothing Norse in their language. . . .

"They weave cloth of cotton. Their pottery is made with marvellous skill. They make brilliantly colored dyes from the substances of plants, and they use it for cloths and paintings and potteries, as the Egyptians did."

"And their appearance?" asked Colon.

"They have a reddish complexion . . . of dark shades the color of cinnamon. Their hair is straight and black and shining. There is almost no hair on their bodies. My hairy arms, the waves in my hair, and my thick, curling beard and mustache, amazed them. When I took off my shirt to bathe they were astonished at the hair on my chest. Their cheek bones are high and their eyes slanting. There is something almost Moorish about their noses, which are large and strong yet handsome. They have narrow foreheads."

"How do they live?" asked Colon. "Do they practice trades and crafts as we do?"

"No, my Admiral, their lives are not as ours. They are

hunters and trappers, skilled in knowledge of the forest. Their tools (and they have many) are chipped from stone. They do not raise wheat as we do, but rather maize, or corn. It is beautiful to see it growing in the fields, tall like sugar cane, but greener and more luxurious-looking.

"I have brought you some of their foods." I clapped my hands. My men carried baskets of strange fruits and plants into the cabin. A pair of brilliant birds, alive and cackling, struggled in the grip of my aide.

"Are these peacocks?" asked Colon, looking at the birds in astonishment. "Are they to be eaten?"

"Indeed, my Admiral," I replied. "I call them by a Hebrew name, *tukim*, or 'turkeys.' They are cooked as we cook fowl. They are not domesticated. The natives trap and hunt them. Their eggs can be used in all possible ways."

The Admiral leaned over a basket and lifted out a long, thin brown stick which seemed to be made of uneven sheets of brown paper rolled and pasted together. "What on earth are these?" he asked.

I smiled mysteriously. Without a word, I took it from his hand, moistened one end carefully, and put it in my mouth. I gestured royally to Hermano, my aide. Hermano held a burning flint stick to the other end of my brown wand, the while I, with great care, sucked air through it. Then out I puffed a cloud of fragrant smoke.

The Admiral stared at me as though hypnotized. The cabin boys turned white with fear. "Fire! Fire!" they shrieked! Down came a torrent of water on my unsuspecting head! So much for introducing tobacco to my shipmates!

After I had changed my clothes and the cabin had been

11

swept dry, I told the Admiral more of what I had learned.

"They make ornaments and jewelry of silver and beadwork such as I have never seen before. Their clothes they make of animal skins, and they wear headdresses of bright feathers."

Colon looked at me curiously. "How did you learn so much," he marvelled, "in such a brief time? And how could you talk with these people? If their language is like no other you know. . . ."

I looked thoughtfully at the wet, shredded cigar stump still wedged between my fingers. "There are many ways, my Admiral, for an interpreter—signs, gestures, sounds, things he does almost without thought or plan. For instance, I say the word 'counting' and then I count aloud on my fingers— 'one, two, three,' and say the word 'counting!' If my listener does not understand, I try again. I might point at some people and repeat the one, two, three again. And at last they do understand.

"Then, when they count in their own language, I listen most carefuly. Then I can go back to my fingers and say 'finger,' and wait for them to give me *their* word for fingers.

"Then I point to my hand, and say 'hand.' And so it goes. They are eager to understand what the stranger is trying to say. They wish to know about me as I wish to know about them, and thus we teach one another."

"Very skillful," nodded Colon. "Very skillful indeed." (The Admiral is a keen-minded man himself.)

If, with God's help, we survive, and some day my journal is read by others, I hope they will not think me conceited. There was a look so full of respect and admiration on Colon's face after we had talked that I went to my cabin a happy man.

Now I feel no doubt that I am valuable to my Admiral and worthy of the great responsibility put upon my shoulders by my people.

And tonight, the feeling grows upon me, stronger and stronger, that this land may be a haven for us, for many reasons. I do not think that this is China. I think that our voyage will prove this. Those who seek a path to the riches of the Orient will use the way taken by Marco Polo.

Though others may fear these perilous seas, the path of the unknown we are following, *my* people can face danger. They are not afraid of the open seas. They have left Spain, headed for they knew not where, in ships as fragile as a child's toy. These strange and wonderful new lands, with the huge terrifying sea separating them from the Old World, were meant to be settled by those who have the desire and the courage. We have both.

May the day come soon when my people find peace and rest here. May God be with us.

What Do You Think?

If Columbus was really a Marrano, why do you think he became one? Would you have done the same if you had lived at the time of the Spanish Inquisition? Why did Luis de Torres become a Marrano, a secret Jew? What would you have done?

2

JOSEPH NASI
Within the Palace

AT THE time our story begins, in the middle of the 16th century, the ancient city of Constantinople had the look of a city from the pages of "The Arabian Nights." It was a fairy-tale city; an air of mystery hung over domes and spires, tiny winding streets, palaces and green gardens hidden behind high walls. It was the capital of the great and powerful Turkish Empire, and the most important city of all the Eastern lands. The story of Joseph Nasi, a Marrano Jew driven from Spain during the Inquisition who rose to become the most powerful man in Constantinople, is as wonderful as any Arabian fairy tale; perhaps even more wonderful, because it is true. But let us begin.

Night had fallen on Constantinople. In the home of Moses Hamon, physician to the Sultan Suleiman II of Turkey, two men bent over a map of the world. In the lamplight, the tall, thin body of Joseph Nasi, dressed in the clothes of an Italian merchant, cast a long shadow on the wall. Dr. Hamon (for it was he) drew his chair closer to the light. He wore the white turban and flowing robes of the Turkish court.

"Moses, my friend" said Joseph Nasi, his dark eyes fixed on the map, "if the Sultan hears your plea with favor, and if he opens the doors of Turkey to our people, do you know what this may mean to us? It has been more than a hundred years since the Inquisition began and the Jews were driven from Spain . . ."

Moses' fine face was sad. "Indeed Joseph, I know very well what it may mean. All the doors have shut upon us, one by one. Portugal, England, France—and now, from what you tell me, the Inquisition has spread to Italy. Those of us who were able to escape from Spain alive still wander wearily through the world, and no one will let us make a home in any land. Those Jews like myself, whose fathers were lucky enough to find their way to safety here in Constantinople, always feel this sadness. We will do anything within our power to help you settle here. The Sultan will hear our case as soon as I am able to gain an audience with him . . ."

"But remember, Moses," Joseph interrupted, "the Sultan may pity us, but he may also feel that hundreds of penniless, homeless Jews may merely add to the problems of ruling his country. He must understand that, though we have been without roots in any country since we left Spain, we bring with us knowledge and riches. We have much to give to his country.

"For example, there is my own family. For generations we have been bankers who have traded with every country in the world. Dona Gracia, who is head of our family, through her wisdom was able to take much of our vast wealth out of Spain and Portugal."

Joseph lowered his voice. "And even now, as the hatred and destruction of the Inquisition spread through Italy, where we live, she has managed, secretly, to smuggle huge sums out of Venice. We will bring the Sultan our money and our knowledge of the commerce of the countries of Europe."

"Ah, Dona Gracia!" said Moses. "Her beauty, her wisdom, and her courage are known everywhere, even in Constantinople. She has charmed princes, queens, kings. Is it true that she fled from Amsterdam because the Queen of the Netherlands became angered when Dona Gracia refused to permit her daughter, Reyna, to marry a member of the Dutch court, because of her loyalty to Judaism? I heard . . ."

"Yes, yes," Joseph answered, smiling, "but we will talk of that later. But now—look at the map." Joseph's slim, strong hand circled a thin neck of water on the map. "Look, Moses. Here is the city of Constantinople, built on the southern tip of the Bosporus, the narrow strait which connects Europe and Asia. Many ships pass to and fro, laden with spices, fine cloth, and jewels. Our people are bankers and traders, and we can bring riches and trade to Turkey, just as we did to Spain."

Moses nodded, stroking his graying beard thoughtfully.

"You are right, Joseph. It would be a blessing for our people, and an excellent thing for the Sultan, too. I shall plead with the Sultan for mercy and friendship. But I shall show him too that both the Turks and the Jews will prosper."

"We must move swiftly," Joseph stood up. His dark velvet cloak shimmered as he flung it over his shoulders. "I must return to Ferrara at once. Every day the danger in Italy grows greater."

For a moment the two men stood in silence, praying wordlessly that God might move the heart of the Sultan to admit the exiles to Turkey.

"Before I leave, Moses," said Joseph, and suddenly his dark serious eyes danced for a moment, "there is one more thing I should tell you . . ."

"Yes?" Moses answered.

"It is true that Dona Gracia's daughter, Reyna, is as beautiful and charming and courageous as her mother. She hopes that some day we may be free to live as Jews—and that some day she and I may be married. This is the dream of my life. And this, too, depends upon your talk with the Sultan."

Moses clasped Joseph's hand in his. "Go in peace, Joseph, my friend. God be with you. I shall do my best."

"God be with you, Moses." The lamp flickered, and Joseph was gone.

Sultan Suleiman II listened to his friend, the good Doctor Moses Hamon, and understood at once that the Jews could be of great help to the Turkish Empire. He demanded that the government of Venice release Dona Gracia Mendes and her family at once, and that her fortune be returned to her. The Italians did not dare refuse what the powerful Turkish ruler demanded. The Mendes family left Italy unharmed.

Many Jews seeking homes soon settled in Turkey. Dona Gracia and her family moved to Constantinople. Dona Gracia, through her goodness and devotion to learning, became the most loved Jewish woman of her time.

Joseph and Reyna were married, and they too settled in Constantinople, in a house high on a hill overlooking the towers and domes, the winding streets and the hidden gardens.

Soon after his arrival in Constantinople, Joseph was presented to the Sultan. The two men liked each other at once. The Sultan was impressed with Joseph's knowledge of the men and governments of Spain, Portugal, France, England, the Netherlands, and Italy; and encouraged him to expand his family's trade and banking business.

But the Sultan found, too, that he and Joseph had other important things in common. A love of learning and the sharing of one's wealth with those in need mean much in the religions of Judaism and of Islam, which was the religion of the Sultan and his subjects. He was delighted to learn that Joseph was bringing scholars and students to Constantinople, and was deeply impressed when Joseph described the custom of ts'doko. Because of this custom, the Nasi family always set aside a portion of their money for the poor.

The knowledge of international affairs Joseph had gained through banking was of great help to the Sultan, and he very soon came to trust Joseph completely and to lean upon him

18

for advice in dealing with the nations of Christian Europe. Joseph rose swiftly in power and influence. The Sultan always received him alone in a private chamber when they discussed affairs of state, and within a few short years, Joseph stood so high in the Sultan's favor that the French and Venetian ambassadors who had treated his family like wretched outcasts were afraid of his power.

One day Suleiman sent for Nasi in great secrecy. Inside the Sultan's private chamber, Joseph bowed before him.

"Why have you sent for me, my Sultan?" he asked.

"I have an errand of grave importance for you, Joseph," he replied. "There are things which are being plotted in my court that do not please me. As you know, I have several sons, but the rightful heir to my throne is Selim, my eldest. There are many in my court, however, who favor one of my younger sons. I wish to send Selim a gift of great value, to help him now and to warn all those who scheme against him that I will protect his right to the throne."

"What is it you wish? How can I help? If it is within my power, you know you have only to ask and it is done."

In the Sultan's private chamber stood two large chests made of dark, richly polished teakwood, banded with iron and fitted with great, heavy locks.

The Sultan took a ring of huge keys from an inner pocket of his robe. He unlocked the first chest and lifted the lid.

Joseph caught his breath. The chest brimmed with golden coins.

"Here are fifty thousand ducats for my son, Selim," the Sultan said in a low voice. "It is a royal fortune, suitable for my rightful heir and the future ruler of this Empire."

19

The second chest was unlocked. Joseph was almost blinded by the brilliance of hundreds of precious gems; diamonds, rubies, emeralds, pearls and sapphires flashed and glowed with the beauty of rainbow and flame.

Joseph was speechless with wonder.

The Sultan locked the chests. "The gems have a value of thirty thousand ducats," he said. "These treasures are a token of my love and respect for Selim. They must be taken to him in Asia Minor. It is a long, dangerous journey. You will cross the straits and proceed by wagon train to my son. I trust you completely. May Allah speed your journey."

That very night, in secret, Joseph swiftly prepared for the trip. Only Dona Gracia and Reyna knew of his mission. The next morning he set out. His horses sped over rutted roads and dangerous mountain passes. Within a week he stood before Prince Selim, the chests of treasure at his side.

The young prince was delighted to greet the friendly messenger from his father. He took the keys from Joseph and clasped his hand.

"I thank you for the faithful service you have done my father and myself," he said. "In gratitude, I make you a member of my guard of honor, the famous Mutafarrica. And some day, when I am ruler of Turkey, I shall give you lands and a title. It is my hope that you will serve me as you now serve my father."

Joseph and his company rode swiftly back to Constantinople and went directly to the Palace. In the Sultan's private chamber, he gave him Selim's thanks and greetings.

"Joseph, my friend, how can I repay you?" the Sultan

asked. "You are my most trusted servant. I know that you are rich, but surely there must be something I can do for you. Speak, Joseph. I wish to reward you."

Joseph bowed his head, and when he raised his eyes they were bright with unshed tears. He spoke slowly.

"You know well the troubles of my people, my Sultan. Many Jews still flee from Christian lands, hunted and homeless. We have long hoped that our people might rebuild the ruins of the land of our fathers, the holy land of Palestine. You are the ruler of that territory. I ask nothing for myself. But a piece of land in Palestine, where Jews might settle and build new homes, is truly the deepest desire of my heart." And Joseph stood before the Sultan, his eyes lowered, silently.

The Sultan rose from his pillow. "It shall be as you wish, Joseph. I grant you a portion of land in Palestine which includes the city of Tiberias. It is my will that it be settled by Jews, and that you do all that you can to help them live there in freedom and in peace."

The tears in Joseph's eyes were tears of joy as he thanked the Sultan and rushed to tell Reyna the wonderful news.

But, alas, not even Joseph was rich enough to buy all the ships, tools, building materials, stores of food, and stocks of plants and animals needed to settle the lands surrounding Tiberias and to rebuild the ancient city from its ruins. Joseph and his poor fellow Jews must wait. The great plan was still a dream.

In time Sultan Suleiman II died, and Joseph mourned for his friend. Selim now ruled Turkey. As had his father, Selim trusted Joseph with the great responsibility of dealing with leaders of other countries.

But there were men at Selim's court who were jealous of Joseph, who resented his influence over the Sultan, and plotted and schemed to turn the new Sultan against him. One enemy told Selim that Joseph was not to be trusted, that he had betrayed the secret affairs of Turkey to their ancient enemies, the Pope in Italy, the King of Spain, and the Duke of Florence. The French ambassador at the court of Selim also wished to harm Joseph. He believed that if Joseph were stripped of his power the Sultan would deal more favorably with those nations, such as France, which had driven the Jews out of their lands.

One evening, as Joseph was leaving the Sultan's chambers, a friend at the court stealthily slipped a piece of paper into his hand. "I don't know what this means," the friend whispered, "but I think it is suspicious. It is a copy of a strange dispatch the French ambassador has just sent the King of France."

At home, Joseph lit a candle, locked the door to his study, and spread the creased paper out upon his desk. There were no letters on the page, only numbers, which looked like this:

19-15-15-14 20-8-5 5-14-5-13-25 15-6 6-18-5-14-3-8
9-14-6-12-21-5-14-3-5 1-20 20-8-5 3-15-21-18-20
15-6 20-21-18-11-5-25 23-9-12-12
2-5 16-21-20 20-15 4-5-1-20-8

"What on earth does this mean?" Joseph wondered aloud. "It must be some kind of code." He studied the paper. "Now let me see . . . If the numbers stood for letters of the alphabet . . . what would we have?" Slowly, carefully, he went through the alphabet, changing numbers to letters. Gradually the message began to take shape. "Soon," the decoded letter read, "the enemy of French influence at the court of Turkey will be put to death."

"Aha!" Joseph exclaimed. He struck the desk with the palm of his hand so angrily that the candle almost fell on the floor.

"Of course! It is *I* who am the enemy of French influence! Evil men are inventing lies about me, in hopes that the Sultan will remove me from office and have me put to death!"

Swiftly Joseph returned to the palace and asked for an audience with the Sultan. Selim listened quietly as Joseph described the plot against him and showed him the note in code written by the French ambassador.

"It is not true, Selim," he said, angrily. "I have given no secrets to foreign powers. I serve you faithfully, my Sultan, as I did your father before you."

Selim smiled at Joseph.

"I know, my friend. These plots are hatched in jealousy and fear. I trust you completely, and only await the proper time to clear my court of this nest of liars. Perhaps—yes! This may be the perfect opportunity to keep the promise I made you, so many years ago, when you brought me the chests of treasure. Remember, Joseph? Lands and a title I promised you, and lands and a title you shall have! This will be a warning to those who plot your downfall at my court!"

Majestically, Selim rose.

"Summon the court," he commanded his servants.

The room filled with people. The faces of Joseph's enemies were smug and smiling. This, they thought, was surely the moment they had waited for so eagerly—the Sultan was about to dismiss and dishonor his proud Jewish friend! But their smiles vanished as the Sultan spoke.

"Joseph Nasi, I summon all men to hear that I reward your loyal service to our land by naming you Duke of Naxos. You are now Lord of Andro, ruler of the Cyclades in the Aegean Sea. With this title go all the lands and rights which belong with it. Go in peace, my good friend, and may Allah bless your rule."

Joseph lifted his head and spoke proudly for all to hear. "I shall try always to deserve your favor, my Sultan."

He turned and looked directly at his enemies. "Now that I am Duke of Naxos, I shall have the power to rebuild the land in Palestine which your father gave me. And Tiberias will become a center of Jewish life in the Holy Land!"

Dusk was falling on the ancient city of Constantinople, as softly as a silken scarf. The last rays of the sun touched the fig trees and gilded the pomegranate blossoms flowering in Joseph Nasi's garden, high above the mysterious, winding city. They touched the faces of Joseph and his friend, Moses Hamon, as they sat quietly in the fragrant, gathering darkness.

Suddenly, Joseph bent over a tiny, dwarfish tree which grew near the fountain bubbling in the garden. He picked a branch carefully, and held it up in the fading light. It was a graceful little branch, with leaves of dark green. Between the leaves grew small white berries.

24

"Do you know what this is, Moses?" asked Joseph, turning the branch slowly between his slim strong fingers.

The two men bent over the table, intent on the little branch, just as, so many years before, they had bent over a certain map in the flickering lamplight.

Moses examined the leaves and berries carefully. "No," he said, "I don't think I've ever seen that particular plant before."

Joseph smiled affectionately at his friend. "I'm not surprised. It has travelled all the way from China, this little branch. But it has one more journey to make—to Palestine. And there it will become a very important little branch indeed."

"Important? For Palestine? But—why?"

"Forgive me, my friend—I was merely trying to introduce you to that unimportant-looking little tree with the dignity it deserves. Much has happened, as you know, in Palestine, and so quickly! Within the space of one short year, the walls of Tiberias have been restored and new stone houses have risen from the ruins. Our ships have brought many Jews from Italy to our ancient homeland. The Sultan has helped us through his friends in Tiberias, and Dona Gracia has generously given us money."

"I know" said Moses. "And from your college for Jewish students here in Constantinople you have sent scholars, and from the Hebrew printing presses you have sent books—and Torah is once more being taught. But the *tree*, my friend—the tree?"

"People need more than schools and houses and books, Moses. They need industry so that they may earn their own living in the future. In Italy our people grew silkworms and

25

manufactured silk. Silk, Moses, the most precious of all cloths, the most valued! This little tree is a white mulberry, upon which silkworms feed. I have sent hundreds of these baby trees to Palestine. For five weeks, silkworms feed upon the leaves, and then they spin their cocoons. Our people know how to unwind the long, fine threads of the cocoons. I shall send them looms and they will make silken cloth to send to other countries in exchange for goods they need. And they will make wool, too, from the sheep we are raising near Tiberias. But these little trees, Moses, are the beginning of the future.

"Oh Moses, it is the joy of my life to know that in the dark world about us, there is a little circle of light and hope in the Holy Land."

"It is you who lit that light," said Moses, quietly, "so many years ago. Blessed is God who is good and who does good. And blessed are you, Joseph Nasi, servant of the Most High at the court of the Sultan of Turkey."

And darkness fell, quietly as a curtain, on the ancient city of Constantinople.

What Do You Think?

Why was it so important for the Jews to move to a place where they were free to keep their religion rather than stay in a country where they had to keep it a secret?

Something For You To Do

Make believe you are Joseph Nasi. Write the letter telling the Jews that they can come to Tiberias. Also, decide how you can get this letter to the Jews of Spain, Portugal and Italy without the governments of these countries finding out about it.

You'll Enjoy Reading

"The Rabbi and the Inquisitor," *Treasury of Jewish Folklore*, by NATHAN AUSUBEL, Crown Publishers, p. 36.

"Rabbi of Tortosa," *Heaven on the Sea*, by SULAMITH (Ish-Kishor), Bloch Publishing Co., p. 153.

"The French Ambassador Takes a Walk," *Giants on the Earth*, by DEBORAH PESSIN, Behrman House, p. 9.

"A Place of Refuge," *Watchmen of the Night*, by BETTY KALISHER.

"Hail the Duke," *The Great March*, Book II, by ROSE G. LURIE, Union of American Hebrew Congregations, p. 46.

Some More Facts About JOSEPH NASI

Joseph Nasi was born into a wealthy Portuguese Marrano family at the beginning of the sixteenth century. He received training in banking in Antwerp, Belgium, but could not bear to pretend that he was a Christian. Nasi decided to go to Turkey and accept the freedom offered by Sultan Suleiman.

On the way, Joseph's aunt, Gracia Mendes, was imprisoned in Venice on charges of practicing Judaism. Suleiman demanded her release and helped his new subjects to settle in Constantinople.

Joseph prospered. His influence went even as far as Holland, where William of Orange asked his advice. King Sigismund August II of Poland, too, sought Joseph Nasi's counsel.

When Venice was crippled by a great fire in 1569, it was Joseph who urged Sultan Selim to seize the island of Cyprus. For this suggestion, Joseph was made governor of Wallachia.

Joseph Nasi died in 1574.

3

RABBI MANASSEH BEN ISRAEL
Portrait of a Dream

THROUGH the high studio window the foggy, grey-gold light of Amsterdam fell softly on the painter and his subject. Rembrandt's palette was heavy with rich, deep pigments, and the canvas upon which he was working was swiftly coming to life under his short, firm strokes. His subject, Rabbi Manasseh Ben Israel, dressed in a large hat and white-collared, long, black robe, sat facing him, his head turned slightly to one side. A coal fire glowed red in the fireplace. The studio was piled with heaps of books and canvases. Paintings leaned helter-skelter against walls and chairs.

Rembrandt's strong shoulders moved rhythmically be-neath his blue smock as he worked. His dark eyes, deep-set under their bushy eyebrows, were intent on the face of his friend.

The Rabbi rather liked having his portrait painted. It was not a new experience for him; Rembrandt had sketched him many times. He enjoyed watching the artist work. And Manasseh was proud that Rembrandt had illustrated the Rabbi's own books with his marvellous etchings.

Manasseh turned his open, compassionate face toward Rembrandt.

"Tell me, my friend, why have you taken a house here in the Jewish section?" he asked. "Very few of our Gentile neighbors care to live in our part of the city."

The painter studied Manasseh's face closely and made a quick brush stroke on the canvas.

"A painter needs life and color around him. To an artist this is the most interesting part of the city. Every ship brings newcomers, new types, new faces. Here I meet writers, scholars, poets from everywhere. And where else in Amsterdam do people speak Spanish and Portuguese? The Jewish quarter is bursting with activity. And you, Rabbi—what brought you here to Amsterdam? I am curious."

Manasseh smiled. "It is a long story, my friend. I was born on the Portuguese Island of Madeira. My parents were Marranos who had been forced to deny their Jewish faith. I was baptized—yes, baptized!—Manoel Dias Soeiro, named after my Christian godfather. But despite these efforts to conceal our faith the Inquisition drove my family to France —the persecution spread to France, and we fled to Holland. Here, at last, we Jews were free to be ourselves. My father at once threw off the cloak of Christianity and declared his faith openly. And he renamed me Manasseh, which, in Hebrew, means 'God hath made me forget my toil.'

"I live here because it is one of the few places in the world where my people are free from persecution. And in these years I have come to love this low country, its canals, its dikes, its windmills—even its rain and fog. This is truly my home—the only one I have ever known."

Rembrandt put down his brush. "Tell me, Rabbi Manasseh," he said, "how did the first Jews come to Holland?"

Manasseh relaxed his pose, crossed his legs, and stroked his beard.

"When the Jews knew that the Dutch were free, at last, of Spanish rule, they came, for they knew that here they could worship God freely. Holland is one of the few countries where religious freedom is permitted to us.

"Before they were safely settled in Holland, however, many of our fugitive Marranos had strange, harrowing adventures. One group, fleeing from Lisbon, was captured by an English ship and taken to port. Among them was a young woman named Maria Nunez. She was wonderfully beautiful, beautiful in a way which is rarely seen. The English nobleman in command of the ship was fascinated by her beauty and wished to marry her."

"I wish I could have painted her," Rembrandt said.

"Well, he took her to London, so the story goes, where Queen Elizabeth, hearing the story, insisted on meeting the beautiful captive. The Queen, too, was charmed by her loveliness; she drove with Maria through the streets of London, and ordered that the ship and all its passengers be set free. Though she had many tempting offers, Maria would not stay in England, where she could not freely practice her faith. The Marranos, and Maria, were at last permitted to leave England and found their way to Amsterdam. Later, Maria married one of her fellow Marranos who had escaped with her—it was the first Jewish wedding ever to take place in Amsterdam. Imagine what this freedom must have meant to my people! We bless the soil of this country."

"But this is as it should be," said Rembrandt. "Men need different kinds of religions. It saves them from imagining that there is only one way to reach God. And your people have been of great help to the Dutch, too. You have helped us develop our trade and commerce, so much so that we have the greatest empire and the largest navy in the world. We have much to thank you for."

The Rabbi sighed. "But Holland is a small country. There are still so many Jews who seek a safe place to live."

"What about England, Rabbi? It is not a Catholic country. The Inquisition cannot reach your people there."

The Rabbi's face lit up. "England is very much in my thoughts these days, my friend. Since 1290, when we were driven from that country by Edward the First, we have wished to return there. Now that England has a more democratic form of government under the Commonwealth and the Lord Protector, Oliver Cromwell, the English may think more kindly of allowing us to return.

"The day may yet come, Rembrandt, when I shall go to England and ask its new leaders to let my people settle there and live their religious life freely. If ever this dream succeeds, it will be because I shall be able to point to the example of how well the Jews get along with their neighbors here in Holland." Manasseh walked home, deaf to the noises of the busy streets, deep in thoughts of England.

In the busy years that followed, Rabbi Manasseh ben Israel never forgot his dream of a Jewish settlement in England.

Manasseh was, perhaps more than any man of his time, the person to whom the English might lend an ear on behalf of Jewish settlement. He was a rabbi, an author, a book publisher, and a merchant trader. He had built the first Hebrew printing press in Holland, and because of this Amsterdam became the center of Jewish book publishing and learning. At the Yeshivah, where he taught, he was a teacher of Baruch Spinoza, who was one day to become one of the greatest thinkers of all time. Despite his scholarship and his many interests, the Rabbi somehow found time to write a book in Hebrew, which he then translated into Latin (for he was also a great Latin scholar) called the "Hope of Israel" which he dedicated to the English Parliament. The book set forth his ideas and his hopes for the Jewish people.

It is not surprising that, after some years of correspondence with Manasseh, Oliver Cromwell, Lord Protector of the British Commonwealth, invited him to come to England for a conference of statesmen, scientists, and religious men meeting to consider the admission of Jews to England once more. Thus it was with high hopes that Manasseh, dressed, as always, in his large hat and long black robe, walked through the crowded, noisy streets of London at the side of his friend, Oliver Cromwell. The Conference had gone on for many weeks, but no agreement had yet been reached on the admission of the Jewish people to England. But Manas-

Manasseh walked through the crowded, noisy streets of London at the side of his friend, Oliver Cromwell.

seh was not discouraged; he understood full well that Cromwell knew the Jews could bring their wealth and knowledge of trade and banking to England, and could, as they had in Holland, help the country to become rich and powerful.

"I do not understand," said Manasseh, as the two men threaded their way through the bustling streets, "why these worthy gentleman cannot come to an agreement."

"My friend" said Cromwell, running his hands through the long hair which flowed over his starched collar, "it is a difficult situation. There are silly stories about your people circulating, and ugly rumors spread like wildfire. Some say that since you visited the libraries at Oxford and Cambridge Universities, you plan to buy our libraries and St. Paul's Cathedral as well. They even pretend that you will try to convert the English Protestants to your religion."

Manasseh smiled patiently. "Your Excellency," he said, "these stories are ridiculous. I hope that your Conference will see through such nonsense. We seek a home for our people in England because we are poor and in exile, nothing more. We wish to remain true to our religion, even as you do to yours. This is all we ask. You know that."

Cromwell nodded, thoughtfully. "Indeed I do. But come. Let us see what today's discussion will bring."

Inside, the Conference was noisy and angry; the crowd hooted, stamped, and booed, and, from time to time, men leaped upon the tables and hurled arguments and heated words at one another. It was a scene of utter confusion and disorder.

At last Cromwell could stand no more. He leaped to his feet and slapped the table with his fist.

"The Conference will come to order!" His voice rang out over the din and confusion. "Those who cannot keep the peace will be taken into custody by the police and thrown into the dungeon. Quiet! Quiet while I speak!"

Silenced by the Lord Protector's anger, the Conference members and visitors returned to their seats. A hush fell upon the room.

"Now, hear this," Cromwell said, in a voice which reached every corner of the crowded hall. "When I called this Conference, I told you that there were only *two* questions for you to decide—*nothing more.*

"First—is it legal for us to permit the Jews to settle in England? You reached the answer to this question at once. There is no legal reason in our Constitution for keeping Jews out of England if we wish to admit them.

"Second—if it is legal, which you have decided it is, on what terms should we admit them? What special taxes should they pay and what will be their rights when they do settle here? Shall they be treated as ordinary Englishmen, or shall they be forbidden to hold certain offices and to enter certain businesses?

"You have been arguing this second question for weeks. I have heard more nonsense here than I thought could possibly be spoken by sensible Englishmen. It is clear to me that I shall get no help from the Conference in settling this second question. The Council of State and I shall have to make our own plans. I have no more time to listen to your foolish bickering. I announce the closing of this Whitehall Conference!"

And Cromwell strode angrily from the room.

The sails were billowing in the early morning sunlight. Cromwell stood with Manasseh while the ship for Holland prepared to sail. The Rabbi looked old and tired. His son, Samuel, had died in England. His plans had come to nothing, and he was sick at heart.

"My friend," said Cromwell, "I hope that you will soon feel better and return again to our shores."

"Why should I come back to England?" asked the Rabbi, wearily. "I have failed. I am a broken man. I return to my home in Holland to die."

"But my friend," said Cromwell, his eyes warm with sympathy, "things will change. They have already begun to. The Jewish families in London are coming out of hiding; they have found a house for their synagogue and have bought land for their own cemetery. The Conference proved that you cannot be turned away from England for any legal reason. . . ."

"Perhaps," said Manasseh sadly. "But I am not so easily satisfied. My people have a proud history, a great tradition. Why must we crawl back to England, like criminals, under cover of night? I wrote and worked and prayed for full, free public recognition of our people and our religion. I have failed. But I shall remember you always as my friend and a friend of my people . . . farewell."

Cromwell stood on the shore, watching until the ship was at last a tiny speck far out on the horizon.

Manasseh returned to Holland broken-hearted. But his efforts were not in vain. Though he never lived to see the fulfillment of his dreams during his own lifetime, the Conference had really accomplished what he had hoped it would.

Once the English government had agreed that there was actually no legal reason which prevented Jews entering England, the Jews began, gradually, to come. And because the Conference had been unable to agree upon the special conditions to be imposed upon Jews regarding how they should be permitted to live and to work, England, in time, gave the Jewish people more freedom than they had ever dreamed possible. The Jews of England became as honored and powerful as they had been in Spain before the Inquisition. The tree of freedom which Manasseh planted bloomed after his death, and keeps his memory alive.

What Do You Think?

If you were Manasseh ben Israel, returning to Holland, would you think that you had failed in your mission?

Something for You to Do

Pretend that you are Manasseh ben Israel and that Rembrandt is painting your portrait. Have a friend act out the part of Rembrandt and make up a list of questions and answers that you can use together.

You Will Enjoy Reading

Watchmen of the Night, by BETTY KALISHER, Union of American Hebrew Congregations, p. 128.
Leaders of the People, by JOSEPHINE KAMM, Abelard-Schumann, p. 102.
The Great March, Book II, by ROSE G. LURIE, Union of American Hebrew Congregations, p. 19.

Some More Facts About Manasseh Ben Israel

Manasseh ben Israel was born in Madeira in 1604. At the age of sixteen he moved to Amsterdam where, two years later, he became rabbi of a new congregation. Manasseh soon built a reputation as one of Amsterdam's best speakers.

To add to the low salary his poor congregation was forced to pay him, Manasseh started the first Hebrew printing press in Holland. He printed a Hebrew prayer book set in a new type, a Hebrew grammar, and a beautiful edition of the Mishnah.

Even printing could not provide enough money to live on. Manasseh was about to leave for Brazil in search of a better job when he was made head of a new yeshivah in Amsterdam at a much greater salary.

Manasseh believed that the Messiah would come sooner if Jews were allowed to settle in countries where they were barred. He corresponded with Protestants all over Europe who believed the same thing and worked towards freedom of settlement for Jews.

Manasseh died in Holland in 1657.

ISRAEL BA'AL SHEM TOV
The Good Master of the Name

OF COURSE I remember Israel, son of Eliezer. Who could forget him? Let me tell you how it was when we were boys growing up together in the little town of Okup, in the province of Podolia, Poland, in the early 1700's.

Our village was not much different from many other small Polish towns. In summer it was hot and steamy. In winter we were shut in by the snow. We used to break icicles from the low-hanging roofs and lick them as we walked to Hebrew school.

But there were two things we had in Okup—a school and a synagogue. Most Jews were simple men, poor peasants, really. Some were peddlers, some split wood, some drove carts for a living. But all Jews prayed, and all Jews studied

Torah. We were poor but we had our school and synagogue.

But if the rest of us were poor, Israel's family was the poorest. His father, who had been a pious and learned man, died when Israel was very young. There was hardly enough for Israel's family to eat, much less any money left over to send him to *cheder* with the rest of us.

But in our little town, when a good Jew died, we all tried to help his family. The neighbors would not let their friend's little boy be deprived of *cheder*. So they all gave something to the *m'lamed*, the Hebrew teacher, and Israel was able to go to school with the other boys.

Israel seemed quite glad to go to school with us. Even now I can see his deep brown eyes shining in the pale, thin face framed with dark reddish hair. His coat and pants were patched so much that one couldn't tell what kind of cloth they were made of, but he did have a pair of stout boots, and I remember how happily he trotted ahead of me through the snow as we marched to school. Yes, my friend Israel enjoyed going to school. But then, he seemed to enjoy everything, with a deep quiet air of being thankful for simply being alive. The trouble was, he did not enjoy staying in school, especially in the warm, bright days of spring and summer. In fact—I might as well tell you now—Israel was just no good as a student. He was absent from class half the time.

At first, no one knew where he went—we didn't find him at home after school. But one fine day in spring, a woodcutter was walking through the green, blossoming woods. And he walked right into Israel, sitting on a log, absolutely still, gazing up through the young green leaves at the warm blue sky and the fluffy white clouds beyond. A fawn sat quietly near Israel's feet, and a grey squirrel chattered on his shoulder. The animals fled as the woodcutter approached.

"Boy," said the woodcutter in amazement, "what on earth are you doing here?"

Israel did not answer. He was lost in his dreams—who knows of what? So the woodcutter took him gently by the hand and led him back to school.

But Israel wandered off again the next day, and the next, and the next. He wandered off so often, that at last the *m'lamed* gave up in despair and told the neighbors that Israel's education was a waste of money.

Well, the neighbors thought, if Israel could not study, perhaps he could work at something? But what could a little fellow do who wasn't even *Bar Mitzvah* yet? Anyway, Israel became a "helper" in charge of escorting the youngest children, little ones five and six years old, back and forth from *cheder* every afternoon.

Israel did this very well, and with great enthusiasm. It was quite a sight to see him lead the little ones to school. The children marched, everyone in step, with Israel at the head of the column waving a stick, while the children sang songs he had taught them. The little ones enjoyed this hugely.

All went well with Israel's new task, until one day something unexpected and frightening happened. As Israel was marching the little ones down a side road at the edge of town, a hungry wolf attacked the children. The little boys screamed loudly and fled in all directions. Some fell and cut their hands and knees on the rough pebbles. But Israel bravely stood his ground, waving a stick and shouting wildly at the wolf. Peasants passing by heard him and hurried to the rescue, and the wolf disappeared back into the forest.

None of the children was seriously hurt, but the parents had lost their confidence in poor Israel and did not want him to take the children to school any more. Israel felt very bad about this indeed, and promptly paid a visit to the families of the boys in his group. Israel explained very carefully that he had replaced the light stick with a heavy club, which might not be so good for leading songs, but was fine for fighting off wolves if ever they attacked again. The parents decided to trust him once more with their children.

Israel did so well as a children's helper that after a while, he was promoted to *shamas* of the school. But as always, Israel didn't quite behave like the rest of us. Whenever we came to the *beis ha-midrash* during the day, there he'd be fast asleep, curled up like a kitten on a straw mat behind a little partition in the corner.

But about this time, I began to suspect that my friend Israel may have known more than most people thought he did, for a very curious incident occurred. Late one night, I returned to school for a book I had forgotten that day. To my great surprise, I saw candles burning in the synagogue next door. This was unheard of; no one was ever in the synagogue this late. I stole in quietly. To my amazement, there stood Israel, alone behind one of the reading desks, bent over a huge Hebrew book. So deep in his studies was he that he did not see me, nor did he answer when I touched him gently on the shoulder and spoke his name. I left, puzzled and confused by what I had seen.

When my family moved to the city of Brody some miles away, I lost touch with him. But two or three years later, Israel turned up. He was a *m'lamed* now, a teacher of young children, dressed in a short fur coat and broad leather belt. No one thought he really knew anything, so they put him in charge of teaching beginners. Israel had changed very little. He was still gentle and warm and a little odd. He studied and prayed all night and went into the fields to think, quietly, whenever he had time. The children loved him.

Imagine the surprise of everyone in Brody when we learned that our unscholarly friend Israel was to marry the sister of our learned rabbi, Rabbi Kuttower. It must have surprised the rabbi too, and shocked him somewhat, for shortly after the wedding he gave a horse and wagon to his sister, and suggested that she and Israel move to some other town. No doubt the poor rabbi was quite embarrassed to have such an ignorant fellow for a brother-in-law. We sympathized with him.

Two or more years passed, busy ones for me. I knew from rumors that Israel and his wife were living somewhere in the Carpathian mountains.

I was hired as steward for the estate of a Polish nobleman, near Brody. Between collecting rents from drunken peasants, and avoiding the fierce dogs my employer kept in large numbers at the manor house, I did not have much time to think of my old friend Israel, and gradually he faded from my memory.

One day, perhaps a year later, my "Pan" (which is what the Poles call landowners) instructed me to ride into the country to look at a piece of land which was for sale, that he wanted to buy. With a careful eye for the dogs, I went to the stable and hitched a horse to a small rig. A click of my tongue and we were off, trotting briskly through the crisp autumn countryside.

43

The narrow road wound higher and higher into the mountains. As we rounded a bend, a completely unexpected scene met my eyes. A ragged man was digging heavy chunks of limestone from a small stone quarry hacked out of the side of a hill. A swaybacked horse was hitched to an old wagon tied to a nearby tree, and in the wagon a woman sat quietly, sewing and occasionally glancing at the man.

It was very strange to come upon this scene in the heart of this rough, deserted mountain country. I reined the horse to a walk as I drew near. There was something oddly familiar about the man. I jumped down from my carriage, threw the reins over a bush, and approached him. The tall, thin figure turned toward me, and I saw his face, burned bronze by the sun and wind, framed in a reddish beard. It was none other than my old friend, Israel Ben Eliezer!

"*Shalom*, Israel!" I cried, seizing his hand. "What on earth are you doing here?"

"And to you Jacob, may there be *Shalom*," he answered in a slow, deep voice, as if not much used to speaking. He seemed to search for words. "My wife and I live near this quarry. I dig the lime from the side of the hill. These are my tools—a pick and a mallet and shovel. I fill the wagon and my good wife takes the lime to town and sells it. God provides limestone that men may use it to sweeten the earth, to build walls, to cleanse that which is soiled. And for me, God has provided it as a way of earning a living. Is it not good?"

"Yes, yes, Israel," I answered doubtfully. "But you are so alone here, so far from the cities. How can you pray where there is no synagogue?"

"Jacob, my friend, I *know* that God is in the synagogue. But He is also here, under the heavens, above the mountains, and in my heart. One does not need to pray in a synagogue, for 'the heavens declare the glory of God.' I live very simply here. Often I fast. When I must eat, I bake water biscuits from the flour my good wife brings from town. But though my life is simple and unlike that of others, I know that God hears me, too. I know that the most ignorant man who truly loves God is equal to the wisest scholar."

"B-but Israel," I stammered, not quite understanding what he meant, but feeling, somehow, that what he said was very important, "How long can you live like this? How can you separate yourself from your fellow Jews this way— will you never return to the city?

"Someday," said Israel, his eyes kindling with an inner fire, "someday when I am ready, I shall return to the city and the synagogue, and the life which other men live. When I am ready.

"But now"—he bent to push the shovel into the broken bits of limestone—"you must forgive me. I must load the wagon." And he turned away.

I drove home through the mountains slowly, thinking of Israel's strange words, and of his hard, lonely life. I did not quite understand my old, familiar childhood friend. It came to me, then, that perhaps none of us had ever really understood him.

At last, as he had promised, Israel did return to town. For awhile he worked as driver for his brother-in-law, but the horses got stuck in a swamp and Rabbi Kuttower decided that Israel was hopeless, and no better at driving than at anything else he had attempted. Finally, because he loved his sister and wanted to see her properly taken care of, the rabbi bought her a small inn to run. And Israel was free to study his mystical books and to pray.

I was at the inn myself one Tuesday when a pupil of Rabbi Kuttower, Reb Mendel, arrived at the inn. After supper I heard Reb Mendel say: "Israel, get the horses ready. I must be off."

As Israel hitched the horses to the carriage, he asked Reb Mendel: "And what if you should find yourself still here at the inn when Sabbath comes?"

Reb Mendel laughed at Israel's question; his destination was just a few hours away—and it was only Tuesday!

"What a question!" He laughed. "I shall be home by Wednesday morning!" And away he went.

But Reb Mendel had journeyed just a mile when his carriage wheel broke, and he was forced to return to the inn for repairs. And each time he started off from Israel's inn, something else went wrong. He was delayed on Wednesday, on Thursday, and on Friday. By Friday night he had no choice but to spend Sabbath at the inn.

It was Israel's custom to stay in the fields until dark, to welcome the Sabbath in the rosy sunset and the deepening blue of the evening sky. Reb Mendel made *kiddush* and sat down to the Sabbath meal with Israel's wife, their little boy Hershale, and me.

Late that night Israel returned. He seemed very far away from us all as he paced before the fire, softly humming Sabbath melodies to himself. Though it was late, he chanted

46

the *kiddush*. And then he sat down and explained the week's portion of Torah from the book of Exodus to us.

Israel's explanation was unlike anything we had ever heard before. It was brilliant, but more than that; he seemed to breathe a new meaning and a new spirit into the familiar words.

The rabbi was amazed, almost stunned. Never had he heard such an inspired explanation of the text. It seemed almost as though God himself was telling Israel what to say.

We sat without moving, listening spellbound to every word. In the glowing firelight, as he talked Israel's face seemed the center of a great light, a great joy. A warmth and peace we had never felt before filled our hearts. We felt very near to God in the humble room of that plain country inn.

At last Rabbi Mendel spoke. "Israel," he said quietly, "what were you thinking last Tuesday, when you asked me whether I might not have to spend the Sabbath with you? Could it be that you somehow knew I would be delayed these four days—that you foretold what would happen?"

Israel did not answer. He merely smiled at the rabbi with great sweetness.

Reb Mendel spoke again. "I am glad I was detained. It is God's will, perhaps. For you are more than a poor innkeeper. You are a true rabbi, *a Ba'al Shem*, a Master of the Name. You must come to the city and speak in the synagogue. In their poverty and darkness, our people need your light."

Israel bowed his head in silent consent.

And Israel did speak in the synagogue, a few days later.

The effect of his words was marvellous. With eyes full of wonder the listeners crowded round him, asking questions, seeking his advice. He listened carefully to them all, and gave each an answer full of knowledge and understanding. And at the end of each serious reply, he would smile and add a touch of humor; everyone who spoke to him felt a great happiness and warmth. He told us to worship God with joy, to pray sincerely, and to live without fear. And everyone, even Rabbi Kuttower, suddenly realized that this man was a learned man, to whom God had given a great gift and a great love for all men.

You probably know how famous Israel, the Ba'al Shem, became. The people followed him through the streets, blessing him and calling him Israel Ba'al Shem Tov—Israel, the good Master of the Name. For twenty years he healed and comforted the poor, broken Jews of Eastern Europe. We shall never forget his kindness. He taught us that despite our poverty and suffering there is joy in living, and that God is in all of us, learned and ignorant alike. His mere presence brought us happiness in the midst of sorrow.

It is a strange story, isn't it, this story of a poor, dreamy, lonely boy, who grew into a great and beautiful spirit?

What Do You Think?

Did Israel Ba'al Shem Tov truly deserve to be called *Ba'al Shem*—the Master of the Name? Why?

What did Israel Ba'al Shem Tov mean, when he said that God is not only in the synagogue, but also under the heavens, above the mountains and in his heart?

48

Something for You to Do

Think of the Bible stories that Israel Ba'al Shem Tov might have liked, when he was a boy. Tell one of the stories and then try to explain why this story would be one Israel would like.

You Will Enjoy Reading

Watchmen of the Night, by BETTY KALISHER, Union of American Hebrew Congregations, p. 136.

Stranger Than Fiction, by LEWIS BROWNE, Macmillan Company, p. 287.

The Jewish People, Book III, by DEBORAH PESSIN, United Synagogue Commission on Jewish Education, p. 99.

Some More Facts About Israel Ba'al Shem Tov

Israel ben Eliezer (called the Ba'al Shem Tov) was born in Okup, Poland, about 1700. He married at the age of eighteen, but his young bride died soon afterwards. Israel settled down as a teacher near Brody.

His wisdom and honesty attracted so much attention that he was often called upon to settle arguments among the townspeople.

After his marriage to Hannah (see the story) the couple lived in great poverty in the Carpathian Mountains of Poland. Israel dug lime. Hannah took the lime to neighboring towns to sell while Israel stayed to pray in the forests.

In 1740 they settled in Miedzyboz, Poland, after living in the mountains for seven years. Here everyone came to hear his simple words.

He taught that prayer should be cheerful, that great knowledge was not the only way to be a good Jew, that scholars should not spend their lives arguing over small matters.

Israel Ba'al Shem Tov died in 1760, but his ideas lived on in the movement of Chasidic Judaism.

5

MOSES MENDELSSOHN
The Boy at the Gate

MOSES knew that he must not interrupt his father. He sat quietly on a high stool, listening to the scratching of his father's pen across the parchment. The sound of goose quill against calfskin was a familiar one to Moses, for his father, Mendel, was a *sofer*, a scribe, who copied out scrolls of the Torah.

Reb Mendel and his family were poor, but it was a great honor to be a scribe. In the year 1743, just as today, this was very difficult, painstaking work. Only the purest black ink could be used. Each letter must be perfectly formed, for a single mistake could spoil a whole section of the scroll. When the manuscript was finished, the sections had to be sewed carefully together with thongs specially prepared for this purpose.

Again Mendel dipped his pen into the inkwell and lovingly formed a few more letters. Moses waited patiently. He was a thin boy, with keen dark eyes set deep in his pale, pinched face. Perched on the high stool, intently watching his father, Moses looked tiny and weak for his fourteen years, for Moses was a hunchback. As a child he had lacked something his body needed for proper growth, and now he knew he would never be tall and strong like other boys.

But despite his misfortune Moses' nature was warm and modest and sweet. He never complained as he trudged along as fast as he could behind the other boys on his way to school. Moses was a brilliant student who spent long hours bent over his Talmud. But, though he was respected as a fine scholar, he was also liked and admired by his friends, for he was as kind as he was learned.

Reb Mendel put down his pen and pushed his yarmelke back on his head. "Thank you for being so patient, my son. I know you have been waiting to speak to me. Now, tell me—what is on your mind?"

"Father" said Moses, eagerly, his eyes bright in his thin face, "I must talk to you about my work at school. Since my teacher Rabbi Frankel moved to Berlin, everything has changed. Now that he is gone there doesn't seem much more for me to learn in Dessau. Oh, Father, if only I could go on with my work, studying with Rabbi Frankel, I know I could learn a great deal more. I want to do that, Father, I want so much to go to Berlin where Rabbi Frankel is now."

"But Moses, my child, how can you go to Berlin? I would

51

gladly give you anything we have, but there is nothing. We are so poor. You know how hard life is for your mother and the rest of the family. I could not pay your way to Berlin. And even if you managed to get there, how would you live?"

There was a bright flush on Moses' pale cheeks. "Father," he spoke rapidly and softly, "I know how things are. I know what you think, that I am too thin and weak to take care of myself properly. But Father, I am not a child any more. I am fourteen years old and much, much stronger than you think. I could walk to Berlin, I know I could! And once there, I am sure I can find a place to live. I can work to earn my keep, just as most of the other students do. Father, please let me try."

Mendel looked at his son with love and admiration. He put his hand gently on the boy's thin cheek and said, quietly: "Very well, my son. I shall talk with your mother."

Moses' parents argued late that night, but at last they decided to let him go, for they knew that his studies were the dearest thing in life to him. "But you will have to wait for summer," his mother said, drying her eyes on a corner of her apron. "You must not start out in the cold and snow."

Moses waited impatiently for the warm weather to begin. When at last the trees began to bud and the air was sweet with grass and spring flowers, Moses knew that it was time to embark upon his great adventure.

His mother took his shoes to the cobbler and had them fixed so that they might last as long as possible. She baked extra loaves of bread and filled his knapsack with food for the long journey. Fighting back their tears, Moses' mother and father kissed him good-bye, and he set off for Berlin.

It is about seventy miles from Dessau to Berlin, which was the capital of Prussia. To Moses, the distance seemed unending as he trudged along, his knapsack slung over his hunched back.

At night he slept in the forest by the side of the road. Twice, he found himself near farmhouses at sunset. He approached the houses cautiously, wary of the barking dogs. Farmers allowed him to sleep in their haystacks.

The days passed slowly. As he trudged wearily on, Moses thought he would never get to Berlin, that the journey would never end. But the afternoon of the fifth day there were more houses to be seen, and coaches passed by, horses pacing smartly, spotted dogs running gaily alongside. And that evening, Moses entered Berlin and found the house of Rabbi Frankel.

The Rabbi was amazed to see Moses. "Come, my boy," he said, "wash your poor tired feet. Then we will give you some supper and put you to bed. Tomorrow I will find you a place where you can live and work to earn your keep, and then you will be able to go on with your studies."

Rabbi Frankel found a place for Moses in the home of Isaac Bernhard, a silk manufacturer. He slept in the garret and ran errands and did chores. But Isaac Bernhard soon discovered that Moses was learned and patient, and gave him the job of tutoring his children. Life became pleasanter for him.

Every spare moment in Moses' day was spent at school, studying with Rabbi Frankel. But gradually he began to discover a whole world of learning, of which Jewish scholarship was only a small part. He discovered German libraries filled with thousands and thousands of books; books about history, science, art, ancient and modern languages, all the knowledge that men have gathered together since the beginning of history. Moses read everything, and little by little the world began to open before his dazzled eyes. He taught himself to read and speak German; in a very short while his German was as pure and perfectly spoken as though he had known it all his life.

Moses knew that no people loved learning more than Jews. But he also discovered that there was a great deal of knowledge which Jews did not suspect existed. Living in ghettos, knowing only other Jews, denied the education of German high schools and universities, the Jews studied only their own books and their own history and languages. Moses realized that his people would only be free if they opened their minds to the history, science, art, and languages of the world beyond the ghetto.

He began to meet other students and teachers. Some had studied at the university. One of these men was Dr. Aaron Gumpertz. Dr. Gumpertz admired Moses' intelligence and curiosity, and guided his growth as a scholar.

Moses was a young man in his twenties when Gumpertz asked him to his home. "There is someone I think you should meet," said Dr. Gumpertz with a smile. "He plays almost as good a game of chess as you do, Moses."

So Moses put on his one good dark suit, polished his shoes, and went. Though he did not know it, this was to be one of the most important nights of his life, for it was the night he met the famous young German poet, Gotthold Lessing.

Lessing and Moses played chess, talked for hours, and became very close friends. They were completely unlike in every way; Lessing was romantically handsome, with long wavy hair, he had been educated at the University, and he was not Jewish. But despite these differences, they admired and respected each other deeply.

What impressed Lessing most about Moses at that first meeting was the pure German style of Moses' speech. "Many of your people are difficult for us to understand," he said. "They do not speak our language. This is a pity, for I feel that the spirit of our times will free them from the ghettos and the persecution which they have endured. They must learn the languages of the countries they live in; they cannot use their freedom properly if they know only the limited world by which they have been surrounded. It is men like you who can help by teaching your people other languages and by bringing them knowledge of the world around them." Moses never forgot this conversation.

As always, Moses continued to work and study. His knowledge and understanding seemed to increase with each passing day. He began to write. One paper he wrote dealt with the subject of philosophy. Thinking it rather a good beginning, Moses gave the paper to his friend, Lessing, to read. But, though they saw each other often after Moses had given his paper to Lessing, Lessing never mentioned it to Moses, nor did he send it back to him. Moses began to wonder why. Just as he was about to write Lessing an angry, hurt letter, Lessing burst into his room. "Moses! I have a surprise for you!" he said, grinning. "What do you think of this recently published work?" Lessing handed Moses a small, beautifully bound leather book. On the first page was printed " 'Philosophical Dialogues', by Moses Mendelssohn."

"Gotthold" cried Moses, "this is wonderful of you! And to think I was angry because you never mentioned my paper! How can I ever thank you, my good, good friend?"

"Do not thank me, Moses. I have done nothing for you. It is the German students and the German people I have helped, if any. Now that your work is published they will learn what Jews are really like, how wise and how intelligent. And you have given them the benefit of your talent—for you have a great future as a writer.

"But," said Lessing, thoughtfully, "it is not enough that the Germans read your work and realize how fine a scholar and writer a Jew can be. More people go to the theater than read philosophical essays. And one day I shall write a play about you, my friend. You shall be my hero. And the world shall know what a noble person my Jewish friend is."

Moses and Gotthold threw their arms about each other for a moment. "I am blessed in my work and in my friendships," Moses thought. "What more can I ask?"

But there was something more which Moses wanted, though he did not yet realize it.

Meanwhile, Moses' reputation as a scholar and writer grew. The Jews of Germany looked to him for leadership. He carried his faith proudly, and was admired by Jews for his piousness and by Germans for his talents and his nobility of character. He was an example of how a man might give something to his own people yet enrich the culture of Germany.

These were busy years for Moses. He kept the books at the silk factory of his old friend Isaac Bernhard, and read, studied, and argued far into the night with his scholarly friends.

But despite his growing reputation and his busy life, Moses was lonely. He had always been shy with girls, because he feared they would not like him, for he was small and hunchbacked. He was thirty-two years old and unmarried, and he longed for a wife and family.

Then, quite by chance, Moses met a young girl from Hamburg named Fromet Guggenheim. She was a soft-eyed girl whose nature was bright and loving. She found Moses so wise, so charming, and so understanding that she paid no attention to his poor crippled back.

Not long after the Guggenheims returned to Hamburg from Berlin, Moses found an excuse for a visit to Fromet. This time he and Fromet greeted each other as old friends. Moses knew that he loved Fromet. He asked her to become his wife. Fromet loved Moses too, but told him he would have to speak to her father. When Mr. Guggenheim asked Fromet about her feelings she said, simply: "Father, I love Moses. He is gentle and kind. He is a great man—but very modest. And his heart and mind are beautiful. I want to be his wife."

And so Fromet and Moses stood beneath the *chupo* and were married. In his happiness, Moses was no longer lonely.

Two years later, the Prussian government made Moses a "protected Jew." Very few Jews received this honor. It meant that, unlike most other Jews, he could move freely about Prussia. He could not be expelled from the city of Berlin without any warning, as were the non-"protected," or "tolerated" Jews. He was freed from paying certain special taxes forced upon other Jews.

The leaders of the Jewish community in Berlin were very impressed by the honor bestowed on Moses. They in turn set him free from payment of all taxes and fees which the Jews paid to their own Jewish community.

Moses knew that his new freedom was considered a great honor, but it really did not mean very much to him. Of course it was nice to be "protected," but what Moses wanted was that *all* Jews should have equal rights with other men under the law. It did not seem fair to him that certain men such as himself should be singled out and given special rights while the rest of his people continued to live in the ghettos and pay huge, unjust taxes to the Prussian government.

Moses' reputation as a scholar and writer continued to grow. His home was a meeting place for scholars, artists and thinkers of all religions, something which had been almost unheard of in Germany a few years before. And Moses continued to be as he had always been; pious, loving his own people, but with his heart and mind open to the world.

The same year that Moses became a "protected" Jew, the Prussian Academy held a contest for an essay on the subject of "Evidence." Moses wrote a paper and submitted it to the Academy. When Lessing heard that Moses had entered the contest, he warned him not to hope for too much.

"But why not, Gotthold?" Moses asked, puzzled. "I have worked hard on my paper. I think it says something important, and that I have a chance of winning."

"But Moses, Emmanuel Kant, who is considered the greatest of all living philosophers, has entered the contest too. You cannot expect to win over him!"

Reluctantly, Moses agreed with Lessing. He was undoubtedly right. Kant was thought to be the greatest thinker of his time, and Moses could hardly expect to compete with him.

A few days the winner was announced. It was Moses Mendelssohn! Everyone was amazed—everyone, that is, except Fromet.

"I knew you would win, Moses," she whispered, as she kissed him. "You are my greatest philosopher."

As Moses grew older, it became more and more clear that times were changing. There was a new spirit of freedom in the air, everywhere. The French and American Revolutions had changed ways of thinking all over Europe, and even in Germany there was new hope for change—particularly for the Jews.

Moses had great hopes for the future of his people. But so often he saw the problem which his friend Lessing had talked about that first night they had met. How could Jews be understood and accepted by their Gentile neighbors if they did not know how other peoples lived outside the ghetto? How could they use the new opportunities of freedom if they could not even speak the German language? Many Jews knew Hebrew, and all Jews spoke Yiddish, but only a handful knew German. How Moses wished he might discover a quick way to teach German to all Jews!

Late one night, after supper was over and the children had been tucked in their beds, Moses sat in his study. His mind was occupied with many things. Absent-mindedly he picked up a pen and, idly, began to scribble on the sheet of paper before him.

Fromet entered the study. She leaned over his shoulder to brush the hair from his forehead and said:

"What are you writing, Moses?"

"Not really writing at all," he said, "I'm just thinking and drawing letters while I think."

She leaned closer and looked at the paper. "But Moses, you *are* writing. Those are Hebrew letters. Only," and she bent closer, "the words don't look like Hebrew words. . . . Why Moses, look at what you've written! Those are the first words of the Bible in German, but you've written them in Hebrew letters! *Why* on *earth?*"

Moses shook himself and looked at the page. "The words of the Bible in German, but written in Hebrew letters? That's right! Fromet! Do you realize what this means? I didn't know what I was writing, but I think this the the answer to a problem that has troubled me for years!

"All Jews know parts of the Bible, especially the Torah and the Psalms, right? Some Jews know whole parts of it by heart. I shall translate the Bible into German but I'll use Hebrew letters! In that way our people will be able to learn the German language very quickly! They'll be able to read any German books they like! This means freedom for them, Fromet! Freedom from the ghetto at last!"

He hugged his wife. "Go to bed, Fromet! I shall be up late tonight!"

And Moses began at once. He translated the Torah and all the psalms into German, using Hebrew characters. The Jewish people read his translations. From there they had only to learn the letters of the German alphabet. Almost overnight, the Jews of Germany were able to read and understand books written in the German language itself. With a few strokes of his pen, little Moses Mendelssohn had pushed open the gates of freedom for his people.

I shall translate the Bible into German but I'll use Hebrew letters!

What Do You Think?

Do you agree with Moses Mendelssohn that it was very important for Jews to learn the German language?

Something for You to Do

Pretend that you are going to interview Moses Mendelssohn on a television program in Berlin. Make up a list of questions to ask him. Have someone act his part and then put on the show.

Show the filmstrip *Moses Mendelssohn: Pioneer in Modern Judaism*, but write your own words for each picture.

You Will Enjoy Reading

"To Seek His Fortune," *Great Jews Since Bible Times*, by ELMA E. LEVINGER, Behrman House, Inc., p. 117.

"The Man Who Broke the Ghetto Walls," *Giants on the Earth*, by DEBORAH PESSIN, Behrman House, Inc., p. 58.

"Out of the Ghetto," *They Fought for Freedom*, by ELMA E. LEVINGER, Union of American Hebrew Congregations, p. 139.

"My Name Is Moses Mendelssohn," by MORRIS EPSTEIN, *World Over Story Book*, edited by Norton Belth, Bloch Publishing Co., p. 360.

"The Fighting Hunchback," *The Great March*, Book II, by ROSE G. LURIE, Union of American Hebrew Congregations, p. 77.

Some More Facts About Moses Mendelssohn

Destined to become one of Europe's most powerful literary figures, Moses Mendelssohn was born in Dessau, Germany, in 1729. He devoted his entire existence to finding truth. Mendelssohn even dared to criticize the king of Prussia. The king, annoyed at such impudence, twice prevented Moses' election to the Prussian Academy.

After Mendelssohn's great success as a philosopher his ideas turned more and more towards Judaism. Whenever Jewish rights were threatened, Moses picked up his pen and wrote. He could now use his reputation for the cause of fair treatment for his people.

Following the death of his lifelong friend, Lessing, Moses heard an ugly rumor—people were saying Lessing did not believe in God. He immediately wrote a lengthy manuscript defending Lessing. In it Mendelssohn told of all his friend's religious ideas. But before his book was published Mendelssohn died, heartbroken, at the age of 56.

6

HAYM SALOMON

Our Little Friend in Front Street

IT WAS a great occasion, that day in 1783 in Philadephia. The members of Congregation Mikveh Israel were dedicating their beautiful new synagogue on Cherry Street. Along the walls tall candles flickered. The synagogue was crowded with people dressed in their finest Sabbath clothes. From where he sat, Haym Salomon saw the Governor of Pennsylvania sitting in the front row. Near him, along the eastern wall, sat fiery Rabbi Gershom Mendez Seixas, his handsome, eagle-like face gentle now with happiness and pride.

The Cantor began to chant another prayer. Haym Salomon settled his slight body back in his seat. He relaxed. "I am so tired," he thought. "We fought so long and so hard for this moment that even though the war has been over for years, I still feel weary. So much has happened. It is so peaceful here, so good to have a chance to remember."

His bright eyes closed. Half dreaming, he looked back on the stormy days that had led, at last, to this Sabbath service.

Haym Salomon had left his native country, Poland, to seek freedom in America. The soil of Poland was red with the blood of Polish patriots, and the country was torn and divided by foreign invaders. Haym brought with him to the New World a vast knowledge of foreign trade, a talent for speaking many languages fluently, and a passion for freedom.

Haym opened an office in New York. From England, Holland, and France his many friends helped him with orders for the exchange of foreign banknotes. They trusted him completely with large sums of money, for he was known to be an honest and responsible broker. Trade between Europe and the American colonies increased, and Haym prospered.

But there was growing unrest in the colonies. Many colonists believed that they should free themselves from distant England. Their anger grew—why, they asked, should they be forced to pay taxes to the English government, a government in which they had neither vote nor voice?

Everywhere, men began to meet in secret. "Down with England!" they whispered, "Liberty for America!"

As though it were yesterday, Haym remembered that sunny, peaceful day when Alexander MacDougall, his big frame slightly bent and his ruddy face serious, entered his office on Broad Street and carefully closed the door behind him. Haym had greeted MacDougall from his perch on a high stool. His desk was littered with ledgers.

MacDougall's blue eyes had lost their usual gay sparkle. "Put down your pen, my friend," he said. "I have news which demands all your attention. You have seen with your own eyes what happened when tyrants took possession of Poland. It is no better here. If we do not strike a blow for freedom now, there will soon be nothing to enter in your ledgers."

Haym leaned forward, listening intently. "Yes?"

"We have formed a new group," said MacDougall "—the Sons of Liberty. Will you come to a meeting tonight in my home? Are you with us, Haym?"

"I am with you, Alexander," Haym answered quietly. He put down his pen and closed the ledger before him. "I shall come for a reason which has nothing to do with these ledgers."

He stood up. MacDougall towered over him like a giant.

"The real reason is the cause of human freedom. This is why we all came here. There is no better place to begin fighting for it."

Stealthily, behind locked doors, the Sons of Liberty met that night. Haym joined their rapidly growing ranks. Plans were made for a secret arsenal of guns and ammunition.

And soon the long, bitter war for American independence began. The British army was driven out of Boston and moved its headquarters to New York. When, in 1776, a huge fire destroyed a large part of the city, British redcoats arrested everyone they knew to be in favor of the revolution.

Haym was arrested as a rebel sympathizer. How well he recalled that black winter night when the British marched him off to the old Sugar House which was their prison. The nights were cruelly cold, and Haym had no blanket, just the coat

How well he recalled that black winter night when the British marched him off to the old Sugar House. . . .

on his back. The rebels huddled together for warmth in the damp, freezing darkness.

The British soon discovered that Haym could be quite useful to them. His knowledge of languages was of great value to the British, for many of their soldiers were hired Hessians from Germany. They used Haym as an interpreter.

But the British had reckoned without the cleverness and loyalty of plucky little Haym. When he spoke to the Hessians in German, Haym did not repeat what the British officers wished him to say. Instead of translating orders for military procedure, Haym said: "Why don't you go home, my good man? This will be a long and bitter war. The Americans will win, and you will be killed or taken prisoner and never see your family again. Leave the British army now, while you have a chance! Go home! Desert!" And many of the Hessians followed Haym's advice, much to his delight.

This was sabotage, and a very dangerous business indeed. Should the British discover why so many of their soldiers disappeared each day, it meant the firing squad for Haym.

Fortunately, however, before the British uncovered his deception, he escaped.

How clearly he remembered that night! He lay shivering on his straw pallet, wrapped in his coat, unable to fall asleep because of the cold. The night was absolutely still and black as pitch. Suddenly, from somewhere, he heard a low whistle. Something was moving up above, somewhere in the darkness. Something was slithering down the wall of the roofless old Sugar House. Haym groped along the rough stone wall and suddenly his hand found a length of thick rope, knotted at the end.

"The rope, Haym, the rope! Grab it!" The voice came from the top of the wall.

Haym obeyed swiftly and silently. The rope was being pulled from the top. Up the wall he went, holding on for dear life, bracing his feet against the rough stones.

At the top of the wall, someone steadied him. He almost fell into the arms of his friend, Alexander MacDougall. "Steady, steady, Haym!" whispered MacDougall. "We must go down again, on the other side. There are men and horses below, waiting for us. We must ride like mad to Philadelphia, at once!"

"But my wife—Rachel—and the baby?"

"They will be safe. General Washington has seen to that. But the General needs you in Philadelphia, desperately! We can talk later. Down you go!"

The two men swung over the wall and lowered themselves on the rope, hand over hand. Below, a little group of men, muskets in hand, waited with horses. Haym and MacDougall ran silently toward them, leaped into their saddles, and galloped off into the night toward Philadelphia.

The years which followed were exciting ones. In Philadelphia, Haym dealt with finance again; but this time he used French and Dutch notes to raise funds for guns, ammunition, food and supplies for General Washington's armies.

Haym was once more perched on a high stool, surrounded by ledgers, when his friend Alexander MacDougall brought a visitor to his office. It was Robert Morris, head of the Department of Finance of the Continental Congress.

Morris lost no time in stating his business.

"I come to you from General Washington, Mr. Salomon. He is well aware of your help in supplying money for our new government and our armies. I know that I may speak freely to you. Our situation is very serious. We desperately need supplies. Our soldiers have great courage, but the bravest man in the world can't fight without boots and without food. We need hundreds of thousands of dollars for supplies. General Washington has asked me to appoint you Official Broker to the Office of Finance of the Continental Congress. John Adams has just gotten a loan from the Dutch. We want you to take charge of the transfer of this money. We need you for financial help and advice. Can we count on you?"

"Of course," said Haym, without hesitating. "I shall do whatever I can."

"I knew you would," said Alexander, warmly. "You have always been a true Son of Liberty."

Haym turned to Robert Morris. "My friend praises me too much," he said. "It is true that I am proud to be a member of the Sons of Liberty. But as you know sir, I am also a Jew, and I know how much it means to be a free man in a free nation. Give my respects to General Washington. I shall go to work on the loans at once."

Haym Salomon served his country in peacetime, too. After the long war was over, the new nation had many severe problems. Very often the members elected to the Continental Congress did not receive their salaries for months. Haym lent them money out of his own pocket and refused to accept interest for the loans, although this was common practice. He was known as "Our Little Friend in Front Street, near the coffee house," who was as generous with money to the new nation as he was brave in defending it.

The Congregation stood to chant the Adoration Prayer together in Hebrew. Haym knew the words and melody by heart. Again his thoughts strayed to the Revolution, and what had come after the long, exhausting war.

A law had been enacted which required that men elected to the governing Assembly of the new Commonwealth must swear that they believed in both the Old and New Testament. Such an oath made it impossible for Jews to hold office. The Jewish leaders in Pennsylvania, Haym and Rabbi Seixas among them, had protested against this law. Were things in America to be as they had been in Europe? Would Jews again be denied equal citizenship and full rights?

But this was not Europe, Haym thought to himself. The men he had met during the Revolution, with whom he had worked, men like James Madison and Thomas Jefferson and James Monroe, would not permit this to continue. All those elected would sit in the Assembly of Freemen, and each man would be true to his own religious faith.

"Why," he thought, "this very service of dedication points the way to the future of Jews in America. Where else could we meet so freely to worship? In what other part of the world would the governor of a state, a Christian, have come to the dedication of a synagogue?"

It had not been easy to raise the money for this beautiful synagogue. Haym had paid a large part of the cost. His generosity had encouraged others to give, and at last the house of worship had been built.

71

As the dedication service ended, Haym's thoughts were of the future. This was merely the beginning for the Jews of America. The country would grow and his people would help it; together, they would bring a new kind of freedom to all the world.

What Do You Think?

Why was Haym Salomon so ready to give his entire fortune to the American Revolution, even at the risk of never getting it back?

Something for You to Do

Prepare a certificate that George Washington might have given to Haym Salomon after the war. Make up the words on the certificate, draw decorations on it, and frame it with cardboard or construction paper.

Go to a bank with one of your parents and find out how much it costs to borrow $100.00 for one year.

See the movie *The Story of Haym Salomon* or the filmstrip *The Story of Haym Salomon*. Do you think it tells the story well?

You Will Enjoy Reading

"The Man Who Gave Everything," *Great Jews Since Bible Times*, by ELMA E. LEVENGER, Behrman House, Inc., p. 122.
"Son of Liberty," *Giants on the Earth*, Part II, by DEBORAH PESSIN, Behrman House, Inc., p. 76.
"For Liberty," *The Great March*, Book II, by ROSE G. LURIE, Union of American Hebrew Congregations, p. 116.

Some More Facts About Haym Salomon

Haym Salomon was born in Poland in 1740. During Poland's war against Russia, Prussia, and Austria, Haym was friendly with

72

the great Polish patriots, Kosciusko and Polaski. During the terrible battles of 1772, Haym escaped to America where he later welcomed his two friends.

During the American Revolution he became Official Broker to the United States Office of Finance. Salomon was also a trusted agent of the French. He helped make it easier for the American patriots to obtain French aid.

Salomon helped pay the salaries of many revolutionary leaders because the treasury could not afford it. Among them were James Madison, Thomas Jefferson, Baron von Steuben, and James Monroe.

He helped friends and relatives in Poland, too. They called him "The Good Jew."

Haym was a sickly person. As a result of his imprisonment in the damp Sugar House Prison during the war, he caught a chronic cold. He died in 1785.

7

JUDAH TOURO
Friend of Mankind

THE small, somberly clad figure of Judah Touro was a familiar sight to the people of New Orleans in the 1800's. He was as homey and as trustworthy as the old town clock in the center of town, and, like the old town clock, so reliable that people set their watches by him as he went to and from his general store.

There was a pleasant, friendly feeling in Judah's store; it was like its proprietor, warm and welcoming in a quiet, steady way. The shelves were bright with gaily-colored cloths from far-off places. Bins filled with coffee beans, sticks of cinnamon, and nutmegs scented the store with rich, spicy odors. Wooden kegs brimming with nails, bolts and screws lined the back shelves, and high up the walls glass chimney lamps caught the light as the doors swung open and closed.

Judah was in his late twenties when he settled in New Orleans. He was born in Newport, Rhode Island. His father had been a famous *hazan*; after his father's death, Judah and his brother Abraham were raised by their uncle, Moses Hayes. Moses Hayes was a merchant trader, and it was under his guidance that Judah became interested in commerce. After an adventurous trip to the Mediterranean as overseer of a valuable cargo, Judah decided that he, too, would become a merchant.

It had not been easy for Judah when he had first come to New Orleans; Louisiana had been under French rule, and there were laws, called the "Code Noir," which the French had enforced prohibiting Jews from living and working there.

But, though Judah was modest and quiet, he was plucky and determined. He opened a small dry-goods store in New Orleans and, despite the feeling against Jews, his honesty and intelligence won him the respect of his customers. When the territory of Louisiana was sold to the United States by France in 1803 and became a state, Judah had already been a respected citizen of New Orleans for several years.

On a damp chilly New Orleans morning in 1811, Judah was stoking the black iron stove in his store when the tinkling of a bell told him someone had just entered. He looked up and saw his friend, a tall, big-shouldered man named Rezin Shepherd.

"Come in, Rezin," said Judah. "Here, let me pull a chair up to the stove for you. How are you? Any news?"

"No news, Judah, but many rumors. There is much talk

75

about another war with the British. They have been stopping American ships on the high seas and forcing American soldiers to serve in the British navy. It looks bad."

"It *does* look bad. This is a grave mistake on the part of the British. It is wrong and foolish. It would be a sad and bitter thing if there were to be war again, just when the country is beginning to enjoy peace and to prosper. But if there must be war, I would serve gladly to defend my country."

Rezin's face was sad. "Yes, it would be only right, though I hope in my heart war will be avoided. We are not married, and it is our duty, you and I, since we have no families who depend upon us, to be the first to volunteer. But let us hope and pray it never comes to that."

That evening, as he locked the doors and windows of the store and walked slowly home, Judah's heart was heavy. It seemed only yesterday that the war for American independence had been won. Was the country so soon again to be torn with bloodshed and struggle?

As Judah and Rezin feared, war did break out in 1812. Just two days before Congress declared war, the British agreed to cease searching American ships and forcing American sailors to serve in the British navy, but the news did not reach America in time. And so there was war.

At first the war did not seem likely to touch New Orleans; most of the battles took place at sea and in distant Canada. But one day, news came that the British were preparing to attack New Orleans. Judah Touro and Rezin Shepherd were among the first men to volunteer for the army under General Andrew Jackson.

Judah was given a uniform with pants that were too big and a coat which hung down to his ankles, and a rifle which looked almost as long as he was. After only a few days of drilling the army marched to the outer limits of the city, where the British attack was expected. Judah's company was stationed quite close to the front line, behind a low wall of sandbags.

Not far away, eight thousand British soldiers were preparing to attack New Orleans. At the break of a cold, grey dawn on January 8, 1815, the shrill notes of the bugle were heard, and the British attack began. Bullets whizzed and whined through the air. The Americans returned the British fire with rifles on the front lines and small artillery pieces from the rear.

Judah and his fellow soldiers crouched behind the sandbags. American bullets were proving too much for the British. In confusion, the British began to retreat, leaving the battlefield strewn with wounded.

"After them! Attack! We must push them further back!" ordered the commanding officer. The soldiers began running and jumping over the sandbags. Just as Judah reached the top of the sandbags, he felt a stinging, burning pain in his right shoulder. He fell to the ground, unconscious.

No one stopped for the little fallen soldier among the first waves of soldiers in hot pursuit of the British. But when Rezin Shepherd, pushing forward with the rear company, spied the small body sprawled out on the cold, hard, earth, he dropped his rifle immediately and ran to Judah's side.

Rezin felt for Judah's pulse. At first there was no sign of life, but at last, ever so faintly, Rezin felt a tiny flutter.

77

"Thank God he is not dead yet, but he is very weak from loss of blood. I must save him!"

Carefully, tenderly, Rezin slipped Judah's slight frame over his broad, strong shoulder. Walking swiftly and easily he carried him to a first aid station behind the lines. The bullet was removed, the wound dressed, and Rezin took Judah back to New Orleans to a hospital.

For several days Judah remained unconscious, fighting for his life. But slowly his strength returned. When, at last, he opened his eyes, the first thing he saw was the face of his friend Rezin Shepherd, smiling at him through tears of happiness.

"How do you feel, Judah?" Rezin asked, gently.

"So much better, my friend. It is only because of you that I am alive."

"Please, let us not make too much of it, Judah. I know you would have done as much for me." Rezin grinned. "But you might have had to find someone to help you carry me!"

The two friends smiled at one another. Judah closed his eyes for a moment. Then he opened them and turned on his pillow to look at Rezin.

"This has made me think of many things I had not considered before, Rezin. I feel as if, through you, God has given me a new life. You are a Christian and I am a Jew, yet, despite the barriers which should come between us, I feel as close to you as though you were my brother. I should like to work, not just for myself, or for money, but to bring people closer together, and to share in some way with others the joy I feel about being alive."

"You must not talk too much, Judah, my friend. You are still weak. But I think I understand how you feel. The joy I feel in having helped you is the joy one feels in having been able to do something for a friend, something which matters.

"But you will be weak when you leave the hospital. I want you to come and stay at our home. I, too, welcome you as a brother. And now I must go."

The war was soon over. Two thousand British soldiers had been lost in the attack on New Orleans. General Andrew Jackson and the American troops had completely defeated the British. But the most terrible thing about the battle was that, just like the war itself, there had been no real need to fight at all. Two weeks before the battle of New Orleans the British had signed a peace treaty with the Americans at Ghent, in Belgium. But the news that the war was over had not reached New Orleans in time to stop the British attack and the bloody battle which followed.

Very soon the people of New Orleans were again setting their watches as Judah Touro, a small, quiet, somberly dressed figure, walked by on his way to his store. But now he took a different route, for he was living at the Shepherd home with Rezin and his mother.

Judah had changed inside also. He looked at the world with new eyes, eyes which had been opened to many things. And, in his quiet way, little by little, he began to change things around him.

Louisiana was a slave state, as were most states in the Union, and it was taken for granted that one should own, sell, and buy other human beings. Slaves did the domestic work at the Shepherd home. But Judah had come to despise slavery more and more. He hated the thought that one human being could own another and could trade him like an animal or a bag of wheat. Judah freed his own slave. But, realizing that freedom alone was not enough, he sent his former slave to school, and then gave him enough money to start his own business. The Shepherd family followed his example, and Judah arranged that their slaves, too, should receive education and support in beginning their new lives as free and equal men.

Judah had a great, deep love for America. He showed it in many ways. He discovered that a monument dedicated to the memory of the brave men who had fought at Bunker Hill could not be built because, in thirteen years, only one man (a Christian patriot named Amos Lawrence) had contributed a large sum of money for its construction. This angered Judah. He promptly sat down and wrote out a check for the same amount as Amos Lawrence's contribution ($10,000, which was in those days a very great deal of money indeed) to be given on the condition that the rest of the money needed would be raised by public support. Thanks to Judah's example, the rest of the money was soon raised, and the monument was built.

On June 17, 1843, the monument was dedicated. In beautiful old Faneuil Hall, in Boston, Judah and Amos Lawrence, two men of different faiths, were honored together for their devotion to their country by Daniel Webster, Governor Morton, and President John Tyler himself.

In the years which followed, Judah's wealth increased. His money was given freely, always, to those in need. When people heard his name they thought of generosity and tolerance for everyone. He gave money to hospitals, libraries, and synagogues, many of which bear his name today.

Though Judah was concerned with the needs of all religions, he was always loyal to Judaism. When he learned that Jews in far-distant Palestine needed help, he sent them large sums of money. When he learned of the sad plight of a newly-discovered colony of Jews in China who desperately begged for help, for Hebrew books, for contact with other Jews in other lands, he instantly sent them money, and remembered them in his will.

But his concern was not only for his own people. Because he believed that all men should be helped, regardless of their race or religion, he gave much money to Catholic and Protestant churches and institutions.

In 1823, a weekly newspaper carried this almost unheard-of notice:

> A Jew! A congregational church was lately sold by auction at New Orleans to pay off the debts of the trustees, and purchased for $20,000 by Mr. Judah Touro, a native of New England and a Jew, that it might be not converted to any other use than that for which it was intended, and the society still worship in it.

Judah had bought the church so that its members might go on worshipping in it.

Judah's business increased until he became one of the wealthy men of his time. As his wealth increased, so did his acts of kindness. There was no worthy cause, Jewish or Christian, to which he did not give his money and his concern.

Though he lived to be almost eighty years old, Judah did

not seem to change much. He still walked to the store every day, his tall, black stovepipe hat on his head, and a scarf and high collar fastened snugly under his serious face.

When Judah died, he left Rezin Shepherd in charge of his estate. Rezin, too, had no family of his own; he added his property to that of Judah, and both their estates were left to charitable and religious organizations everywhere.

He is buried in New Orleans, and on his tombstone these words are cut:

> By righteousness and integrity he collected his wealth,
> In charity and for salvation he dispersed it.
> The last of his name, he inscribed it in the book of philanthropy
> TO BE REMEMBERED FOREVER. . . .

What Do You Think?

Was Judah Touro a good Jew? Why?
Was Judah Touro a good American? Why?
What can *you* do to be both?

Something for You to Do

Draw pictures to go under the following signs which could be used for an exhibit of American heroes:
Judah Touro Fights for His Country
Judah Touro Frees His Slaves
Judah Touro Was a Generous Man
See the filmstrip *Judah Touro: Friend of Man.* Decide which single picture best shows the kind of man Judah Touro was.

You Will Enjoy Reading

"Judah Touro," *Great Jews Since Bible Times* by ELMA E. LEVINGER, Behrman House, Inc., p. 130.

"Judah Touro Spends a Day," *Giants on the Earth,* by
DEBORAH PESSIN, Behrman House, Inc., p. 95.
"He Frees His Slaves," *The Great March,* Book II, by ROSE
G. LURIE, Union of American Hebrew Congregations, p. 142.

Some More Facts About Judah Touro

Judah Touro was born in 1775 in Newport, Rhode Island, the
son of a rabbi. When Judah was twenty-two, his uncle, Moses
Hayes, put him in charge of a valuable cargo to the Mediterranean. It was then he decided to become a businessman.

When Judah went to New Orleans, he did so despite a
French law prohibiting Jews from living there. But Judah was
determined to fight injustice and poverty at all costs.

In 1850 Judah surprised the Jews of New Orleans by giving
them a synagogue. He paid the rabbi's salary too.

After a lifetime of business success and an endless list of
kind deeds, the modest Judah died in 1854. He left $205,000
to give to worthy Jewish causes and $148,000 for Christian
charities.

RABBI DAVID EINHORN

The Right, Always the Right

A COLD sharp wind blew over the wintry Atlantic Ocean and whistled through the wooden buildings of New York harbor. Outside the Customs Building, a little group of four people, their foreign-looking luggage heaped around them, huddled together waiting their turn. The man in the group stood with his arm around a slender young woman with dark eyes and a beautiful, oval-shaped face; his other arm protectively hugged the two little girls who clung to his knees. The man was tall and lean; his strong face was framed by heavy black sideburns. As the little family stood close together, shielding themselves from the wind, the man's dark keen eyes stared at the luggage which was worn and shabby and plastered with many labels.

It was the winter of 1855; the man was Rabbi David Einhorn. He and his wife Julie and their two small daughters had come many thousands of miles, and traveled many weary days, in search of two things which were more important to Rabbi Einhorn than the beautiful green and golden landscape of his native Bavaria, or all the well-known and loved countries of Europe—freedom and progress.

His eyes rested on a battered old black leather briefcase. He had carried it with him for so long, it was like a shabby old friend. It made him think of his student days at the University of Munich. How many years had he carried it with him to classes, to lectures, to discussions of all kinds! It was during those years that he had come to value freedom—freedom of thought, of religion, of speech; and it was there that he had come to realize that progress was part of that freedom, especially for his own Jewish people. He had realized that Jews could no longer live in a ghetto of the mind, and that the Jewish religion too must change; for Jews were becoming more and more a part of the world, in politics, in business and in their daily lives. If they wished to live in the world of free men and still remain Jews, the Jewish religion must change and become more modern. And Jews must fight for freedom of every kind.

At the University of Munich he had begun to fight for Reform; not merely reform in the Jewish religion, but in the synagogues, in business, and in the government of Germany. This did not make him very popular, for Jews everywhere in Europe were still afraid to criticize government and did not wish to see change happen too quickly.

Rabbi Einhorn looked at the old briefcase and smiled to himself. He remembered how hopefully he and his little family had packed their belongings when he had been offered a Reform congregation in Budapest. Reform indeed! Hungary was still part of the Austro-Hungarian Imperial Government, and Budapest was the capital of Hungary. Rabbi Einhorn would never forget his first sermon at the Reform synagogue in Budapest. It was his first and almost his last address to the congregation.

There had been many people in the synagogue that first day. He had preached with the fire of Elijah and the tongue of Isaiah, and he had told them what he had always believed honestly—that Judaism, in order to keep alive, must accept the world of today. Many of the people agreed with him, he remembered; but many feared his ideas. And many feared his brave, courageous criticism of the tyrannical Austrian government.

The Einhorn family had barely unpacked their luggage in Budapest when the Chief Rabbi burst into David Einhorn's study, his face purple with rage. He was so angry he could scarcely keep his voice from trembling. "Einhorn," he said, his voice cracking with fury, "this cannot go on! I will not allow you to speak here! You preach reform, you want to change our Jewish laws! And what is worse, you talk against the Imperial Government! I will ask the government to close this temple! You are a dangerous man!" And the Chief Rabbi stomped out of the study.

And, just as he had threatened, the government closed the synagogue a few days later. Rabbi Einhorn pleaded with the Minister of Public Worship for permission to carry on his religious work, but in vain. The government wanted no new ideas in religion or in politics.

But, though he had no congregation, Rabbi Einhorn and his family stayed in Budapest. He studied every day and began to write a new Reform prayer book. The Austrian government now thought him to be a dangerous man, and the police followed him wherever he went, but he was not afraid. And he continued to think of freedom.

At last he made a decision. One sunny spring day, as he stood with his wife on a balcony overlooking the lovely old city of Budapest, he turned to her and said: "Julie, many young Reform rabbis have found freedom and progress in America. It is time for us to move on. Shall we go?"

Julie smiled at him. "I will begin packing the books," she said.

And now the little family stood, waiting in the cold, wondering what would happen to them in this strange, new country.

In September 1856, Rabbi Einhorn gave his first sermon in the United States at Temple Har Sinai in Baltimore, and the Einhorns settled happily in their new home.

The little family loved the sleepy, gracious city of Baltimore. Life was warm and pleasant there after the frightening months in Budapest. And Rabbi Einhorn found that the members of his congregation welcomed his ideas and wanted a form of Judaism which would permit their children to be loyal Jews as well as loyal Americans. There were no interfering Chief Rabbis and government officials. People were free to practice religion in any way they wished. Rabbi Einhorn loved his new country; whenever he walked through the center of Baltimore, he could look up and see the soaring monument to George Washington, tall against the blue sky, and his heart felt big with happiness.

But the peace and contentment of the Einhorn family was not to last very long. Rabbi Einhorn's long fight for Reform Judaism and for human freedom had, it seemed, only just begun.

Once more Rabbi Einhorn found himself in disagreement with other rabbis about Judaism. Rabbi Isaac Mayer Wise (about whom you will read more later) was a great leader in Reform Judaism. He and other Reform rabbis had met and decided that Judaism should be taught according to the rules of the Talmud. Though Rabbi Einhorn respected and admired Rabbi Wise, and was himself a scholar of the Talmud, he could not agree that modern, American Jews must follow all the rules of the Talmud, for this would force them back into the old, Orthodox ways of thinking and living, which were the very things that had kept them shut away from the modern world. He believed with all his heart that Jews could honestly believe only in modern Judaism and, in order to bring his ideas to many people, he began a magazine called *Sinai*. In it he wrote what he believed; that American Jews must teach their children a modern Judaism which they could understand and love.

And while Rabbi Einhorn wrote and preached his beliefs about Judaism, the storm clouds of the Civil War were gathering everywhere, dividing the North and South against one another. The Civil War was fought because of slavery; the Southern states wanted to continue to buy, sell and own slaves, and the Northern states were against it. When the Civil War began, the Southern states broke with the North and formed a separate Union of States, which they called the Confederate States of America. They refused to continue as a part of the Union, and considered themselves a separate country with a separate government, one which approved of slavery. Maryland, of which Baltimore is the largest city, is a border state, between the North and the South. When the Civil War began there was great excitement and much unrest in Baltimore, for no one was certain whether Maryland would choose to fight to save the Union or join the rebel Southern states.

Rabbi Einhorn hated slavery. He believed that all men should be free and that the enslavement of human beings was a sin against God. Some of the people of Baltimore agreed with him, but others sided with the Southern slave-owners.

Unrest grew in the city. Mobs of angry Southern sympathizers roamed the streets at night, attacking the men and women who opposed slavery. There was danger and violence in the air.

One Sabbath morning the city seemed about to burst like a pent-up volcano. Rabbi Einhorn put down his coffee cup. His face was pale but his voice was steady.

"Julie," he said to his wife, as she untied her apron, "the time has come to speak out very plainly. Every citizen of Baltimore must do his part to keep Maryland from joining the South. We must fight slavery. And every decent Jew must fight it too. And this morning in my sermon I must say so."

His wife looked at him, calmly. "I will come with you," she said, as she hung up her apron.

The members of his congregation must have felt that the rabbi had something very important to say to them, for

Temple Har Sinai overflowed with people that morning. The service was read from Rabbi Einhorn's own prayer book, the *Olath Tamid* (The Eternal Offering). When it was finished, the rabbi rose and stood in the center of the pulpit. There was not a sound to be heard. Rabbi Einhorn stood very straight and tall before his congregation.

"I am very sad on this Sabbath," he said. "Our beloved country is in great danger, not from outside foes, but from enemies within our own borders. Some of you, who still call yourselves Jews, are growing rich on the slave trade.

"As in the case of every evil human condition, some are prepared to defend what is wrong. They go back in the Bible to the time of the flood to prove that slavery is right. Why don't they go back to the Creation, where it says man is created in the image of God, and there is no distinction made between man and man?

"I tell you that slavery is not only a crime against the American idea of liberty and human equality, it is a crime against God. Men and women of Har Sinai, let us rise to the defense of our country! Let us pledge our lives and property to bring slavery to an end!"

Rabbi Einhorn stood silently, looking into the faces of his congregation. Then, lifting his hands, he said quietly: "Let us conclude the service."

That evening, just after sundown, there was a violent knocking on the Einhorn's front door. The rabbi opened it quickly, and young Leopold Blumenberg, a member of his congregation, stumbled in. His hair was wild and the sleeves of his coat were ripped.

"Rabbi," he said, gasping for breath, "you are in great

"Rabbi, you are in great danger. You must leave Baltimore at once!"

danger. You must leave Baltimore at once! The slavery mob has been rioting for several days; tonight it will be worse! You must go! They have sworn to kill you!"

Rabbi Einhorn put his hand on the boy's shoulder.

"What makes you think things are that bad, Leopold?"

"We know," the boy said, breathing rapidly. "We have men planted in the mob. We know they will stop at nothing to force Maryland to the Southern side. They have a list of public leaders in Baltimore who are marked men. Your name is high on their list. They will lynch you unless you leave at once. Rabbi, please, I beg of you, get your wife and the children! We have horses and a carriage. We must leave for Philadelphia while there is still time!"

Rabbi Einhorn tightened his hand on the boy's shoulder for a moment.

"Thank you, Leopold. If I were alone I would stay here with you and face them. But I know that Julie will not leave without me. She would stay, too. I must not let harm come to her or the girls. Wait, Leopold. We will not be long."

In all her many years of traveling Julie Einhorn had never packed as quickly as she did that night in April, 1861. In a matter of minutes the house was locked, the family whisked into the carriage, and the carriage curtains tightly drawn. Leopold cracked his whip over the horses' heads, and off they galloped through the dark streets toward Philadelphia. Behind them they saw the flare of torches lighting up the sky and, in the distance, heard the sound of marching feet.

In a few months the city of Baltimore became once again the quiet, gracious city it had been. Maryland did not join the Southern rebels; it stayed in the anti-slavery Union. The leaders of his congregation asked Rabbi Einhorn to return to the temple, but they asked that he prevent trouble in the future and not speak of "the excitable issues of the time." Though he was homesick for the city where he and his family had been so happy, Rabbi Einhorn could not accept their demands; he knew that to him nothing was more important than the freedom to speak the truth about he problems he saw so clearly.

Reluctantly, he decided to stay in Philadelphia.

But he soon discovered that there were people who respected his courage, and the members of Temple Keneseth Israel asked him to be their rabbi. And the non-Jews, too, were proud to have a man of honesty and conviction among them. They made him an honorary member of the Philadelphia Union League, to which few Jews have ever been admitted.

But the adventures of the Einhorn family did not end in Philadelphia. After the Civil War, they moved once more, this time to New York where Rabbi Einhorn became rabbi of Temple Beth-El.

During the years which David Einhorn spent in New York, many changes occurred in the thinking of other Reform rabbis about Judaism. Gradually they began to agree with Rabbi Einhorn's ideas; and he, in turn, began to understand theirs. In 1869, in Philadelphia, Rabbi Einhorn and Rabbi Isaac Mayer Wise joined hands and worked together for the growth of Judaism in America. When Rabbi Wise founded the Hebrew Union College in Cincinnati in 1875, Rabbi Einhorn became the head of its Committee on the Course of Studies. At the age of seventy, the brave fighter for freedom retired from public life, like a courageous champion leaving the battleground after all the battles have been won. And the Jews of America, from the most orthodox to the most liberal, joined in their praise of his courage and devotion to truth, and his understanding of the future of Judaism.

What Do You Think?

If Rabbi Einhorn were to preach in your congregation this coming Friday night what might he talk about?

Something for You to Do

Suppose your temple decided to buy pictures of several famous Jewish men to place in the hallway and asked the students in the school to make suggestions. What would you say in your letter to convince the committee to choose David Einhorn?

See the filmstrip *David Einhorn: The Father of the Union Prayerbook.*

Some More Facts About David Einhorn

David Einhorn, the father of the *Union Prayerbook,* was born in Bavaria in 1809. He was such a brilliant student that he received his Ph.D. at the age of 20. But because he was so young he could not have a congregation like other rabbis for several years.

David stayed on at the University of Munich and continued his studies, and his ideas turned toward Reform.

Finally, at the age of 30 he began his career as a rabbi with the congregation at Birkenfeld, Germany.

Einhorn was a true liberal. However, the European governments were very much afraid of all liberal ideas. He could not spread his ideas.

After coming to America and serving in Baltimore and Philadelphia, Einhorn moved to New York. Here he found many people who strongly favored Reform Judaism.

David Einhorn died in 1879, having pioneered a new idea against all odds.

9

RABBI ISRAEL SALANTER
For the Sake of Man

SHABOS NOAH, 5621

Dear Yankel:

Now that the holidays are over, and we don't spend all day in the synagogue, I have time to describe our life here in school at Kovno to you. I suppose you wonder how we spend our time? We spend it studying.

It is already getting cold. I feel the first snow in the air. The sky is grey and the leaves are bright with color: yellow, orange, red and russet.

As a student at the Yeshivah, I receive seventy-five kopecks a week as an allowance from a central fund, and that has to last until Shabos. Seventy-five kopecks is very little money, so mostly I eat beans and peas. But on Shabos, it's a different story indeed! The students are invited to eat at the homes of well-to-do families, and several of us are guests of a family named Levinson. At first we used to choke a little— it was hard not to laugh during meals, because Mr. Levinson makes loud, strange noises when he eats. But we soon got used to him. And Yankel, such food! Chicken and kugel and pot roast! Sometimes they give us little cakes for dessert. And there is always a cosy fire burning in the fireplace, and wonderful smells float in from the kitchen.

But enough about food. I'm getting hungry just writing about it. The head of the Yeshivah is Rabbi Israel Salanter. The older boys say that he is a truly great man, that he knows everything there is to know about the Torah and the Talmud. I suppose this is so, but he does do some very, very odd things. He is not a bit like our dignified teachers at home.

Just let me give you an example of his behavior.

One day, my friend Daniel and I went for a walk in the country. We walked along briskly to keep warm, marching in step like soldiers, singing a little song we had learned at the Yeshivah.

> Torah is light,
> Fight for the right,
> Study all night,
> Be ever bright!

As we swung round a curve in the road we suddenly came upon a very strange sight. In the center of the road stood Rabbi Salanter—and a large, sad-looking cow! The rabbi was holding on, doggedly, to the short rope around the cow's neck. The rabbi's shoes and his long black coat were grey with dust.

His broad-brimmed hat was perched dangerously on the back of his head, and his long beard blew in the wind.

When he spied us coming round the bend, the rabbi called "Shalom, boys. Do you know anything about cows?"

"Rabbi Salanter," I said, in amazement, "whatever has happened? What on earth are you doing with *that cow*?"

"What am I doing with this cow? Students of the Talmud should be clever enough to see that it is this cow who is doing something to *me*."

Yankel, we tried, honestly we tried, not to laugh. But we just couldn't help ourselves. Daniel began to giggle. I did, too. Before we knew it, we were both doubled up, gasping with laughter. But suddenly we looked at each other, and we realized what we were doing—we were laughing at the rabbi, and we felt ashamed. So we tried to pretend we'd had fits of coughing, and began to pound each other on the back.

The rabbi and the cow watched us solemnly until at last we quieted down.

"Now, boys," he said, smiling just a little, "I see that the dusty road has made you cough. So be it. If you are feeling better, perhaps you can help me?"

We both nodded, shamefacedly.

"You see," he said, patiently, "this cow belongs to Reb Chernin down the road. When I came along a few hours ago, I noticed the cow had escaped from Reb Chernin's pasture through a hole in the fence and was about to enter the field of a gentile neighbor. This would be considered what the law calls 'trespassing.' As you know, many of our gentile neighbors here in Kovno are not friendly to us. If this cow trespasses in the Gentile's field, Reb Chernin may get into trouble. So I tried to lead the cow back. But, unfortunately, boys, I am not clever with cows, and this cow has no respect at all for learning. Which is why I have had to hold on to her for several hours. You are the first ones I have seen pass by this way."

"Of course we will help you, rabbi." I turned to Daniel. "You hold the cow, Daniel, and I'll cut a switch from a tree."

Daniel took the rope, and the rabbi straightened his hat and dusted off his coat. I cut a switch. We turned the cow around and gave her one smart smack with the switch. Without so much as a backward look she trotted off peacefully, home to Reb Chernin's field.

The rabbi thanked us and continued on to town. We followed him and arrived at the synagogue just in time for Mincho. But what do you think of our rabbi, Yankel?

It has gotten colder the last few days. We were shivering with cold at night, but fortunately Rabbi Salanter persuaded a wealthy man in town to buy new blankets for the students, and it is easier for us now to sleep at night.

But more about the rabbi. He isn't always someone to laugh at, like the business with the cow. Sometimes the things that he does make us feel more like crying.

You see, Rabbi Salanter truly believes people should not gossip. He hates to hear anyone say unkind things about others. Last summer, a woman complained to him that her neighbor was spreading false stories about her. The rabbi begged the gossiping woman to stop saying unkind things, but she was stubborn and would not listen. Rabbi Salanter was so saddened by this that he stopped talking for a whole month! Honestly, Yankel, he would not teach his students nor speak to anyone—except, of course, to God, when he prayed. It made all of us sad, too, when we saw the rabbi going about his daily tasks, with his face set in a look of quiet loneliness, not speaking a word to a living soul.

We felt the same way when we learned what the rabbi had done about the *hekdesh,* the poorhouse. The community supports the poorhouse so that the poor and needy can find shelter and live there until they are able to earn a living. It was very neglected and shabby. Some of the windows were broken, the porch sagged pitifully at one end, and the whole place needed paint and repairs very badly. Rabbi Salanter begged the leaders of the community to repair the poorhouse. But they said that they had no money for it, and that it would simply have to wait.

And what do you think the rabbi did? He went to the poorhouse himself and slept on the bare floor until the leaders of the community promised to make the repairs! We students felt strange about his behavior, but proud at the same time. Our rabbi is not like any other I have ever known.

But sometimes we think he wastes his time. For instance, there was a student here named Samuel. He was not very bright at all, and just couldn't keep up with his studies. He gave up, finally, and left school. He tried to earn a living all kinds of ways, but he simply couldn't seem to do anything well. At last he decided that he would become a *maggid,* a preacher who travels from small town to town, speaking in synagogues. But there were two things wrong with this plan —he had nothing to talk about, and he didn't know how to speak in public!

He asked Rabbi Salanter to help him in his new career. You'd think that a busy man like the rabbi would not bother to waste his time with such a stupid person. But you don't know Rabbi Salanter. Patiently, slowly, he spent hours and hours with poor Samuel. He wrote out sermons for him. Day after day he tried to teach him how to speak to people. After months of this, Samuel set out on his new career, with a briefcase full of sermons (written, of course, by the rabbi), a letter of introduction (from the rabbi) and a sigh of relief (from us). If Samuel had lost the sermons the rabbi had written for him, there would have been one less *maggid*.

But Yankel, let me tell you the strangest story of all. Last Kol Nidrei, Yom Kippur eve, we went to the great synagogue here in Kovno. The sun began to set. The synagogue was crowded with worshippers. Everyone was there—everyone, except the rabbi.

"Where is the rabbi?" everyone whispered in amazement.

No one knew, but we could not wait for him; the service had to begin. The Torahs were taken from the Ark. The cantor sang the Kol Nidrei. The other prayers were recited. But everyone was shocked that Rabbi Salanter had not appeared at the synagogue for the most holy service in our religion.

Toward the very end of the service, just before the Kaddish prayer, we saw the rabbi slip quietly into the synagogue. A buzz went through the congregation. Where had he been?

When the service was over, the president of the synagogue stopped the rabbi as he was leaving and asked in a shocked voice: "Where were you? Such a thing has never happened before—a rabbi absent at Kol Nidrei!"

Rabbi Salanter put his *siddur* away carefully and said, with a gentle smile: "On my way to the synagogue I passed a house where I heard a baby crying. I went inside and found an infant, all alone. A neighbor told me that the mother had put the baby to bed early and left him in order to be at the synagogue in time for Kol Nidrei. There was no one else to take care of the child, so naturally I stayed until the mother returned. Then I hurried to the synagogue."

Naturally, the rabbi, the head of the Yeshivah, the most important man in our town, stayed with the baby! I don't know what to make of it, Yankel. What do you think?

Last summer there was an epidemic of serious illness here. Many, many people were very sick. As usual, there was no place where the poor could be properly cared for. Rabbi Salanter asked the leaders of the community to permit the synagogue to be used as a hospital and lodging for the poor until they were well enough to care for themselves. They said *no*.

Knowing the rabbi, the congregation expected trouble. Sure enough, the next Shabos it came. In the middle of his sermon Rabbi Salanter stopped, pointed a finger at the president of the congregation, and cried loudly: "You will have to answer to the Lord for the suffering of the poor! God would rather have poor Mottel, the carpenter, sleep in the synagogue, than have you pray in it!"

You can imagine what excitement followed! I am told that Rabbi Salanter apologized to the president later, not because he felt that what he had said was wrong, but because he had hurt the president's feelings in the presence of the congregation. Can you understand a man like that?

Before he came to Kovno, Rabbi Salanter lived in the great city of Wilna. I am told that there was once a dreadful epidemic there, too, and many were ill and died. On the fast day of Yom Kippur, Rabbi Salanter mounted the pulpit. As he raised his arms, everyone in the synagogue fell silent.

"My friends," the rabbi said, "Judaism teaches us that human life is precious to God. Many of you have been sick and others are in danger of infection and are weak. It is only right for every Jew to fast on Yom Kippur if it will not be harmful to him or endanger his life. If you are sick or weak, you *must* eat, even on Yom Kippur, to keep up your strength. During this epidemic, everyone must eat." But the congregation did not move. No one could bring himself to break the Yom Kippur fast.

It's hard to believe, Yankel, what happened next. Rabbi Salanter placed a piece of bread and a bottle of wine on the reader's desk and recited the blessings over bread and wine. "Blessed art Thou, O Lord our God, King of the Universe, who brings forth bread from the earth. Amen. Blessed art Thou, O Lord our God, King of the Universe, who creates the fruit of the vine. Amen."

You'll just have to believe what I tell you now, Yankel, even though it sounds impossible. This is what the rabbi did. He knew that the others would not eat unless he set them an example. In front of the congregation, on the Day of Atonement, he ate the bread and drank the wine!

I can imagine your face as you read this. You probably feel the way I did when I first heard about it, or when the rabbi told us why he missed the Kol Nidrei service here in Kovno.

You see, Rabbi Salanter thinks the Torah is for the sake of men, not men for the sake of the Torah. He is trying to make everyone see that the way we act toward one another, how we live with one another, is the most important part of our religion. And more and more, at many of the yeshivahs, they are following his example, and believe as he does.

Well, Yankel, I shall mail this while I still have the money to buy a stamp. Please write to me.

Your faithful friend,
Chaim

What Do You Think?

Imagine that you are Israel Salanter and a serious epidemic threatens your congregation on Yom Kippur. Would you tell them to eat and drink despite the fact that it was the custom and traditional law not to? Do you think that in a crisis there is reason to break some important rules?

Some More Facts About Rabbi Israel Salanter

Israel Salanter was born in Russia at the beginning of the nineteenth century. His real name was Israel Lipkin. But people called him "Salanter" after the city of Salaty, where he had studied under Rabbi Joseph Zundel.

In 1842 he became head of Tom'che Torah Yeshivah in Wilna. He later moved to Kovno, where he established a yeshivah of his own.

The Salanter was a rare person—a very religious scholar who still understood clearly what was important to the average person. He taught that the teachings of Judaism should be applied to everyday life, especially towards the duties of citizenship.

When the Czar of Russia decreed that Jewish boys would be drafted into the Army, Salanter wrote letters to many rabbis telling them to keep records of those who served. Then no one could say the Jews did not do their share.

Israel Salanter died in 1883, after showing Russia's Jewry a new way to practice their religion.

10

RABBI ISAAC MAYER WISE
America Was His Congregation

FROM HIS DIARY
JULY 4th, 1846
On board the Marie
Somewhere on the Atlantic Ocean

July fourth . . . today is a holiday in America. They call it
Independence Day. I have never seen this great new country,
and yet I feel that I know it as well as my native Bohemia.
Truly, I have the American fever.

Theresa and the baby are down in the cabin. Some of our
friends have gone to ask the Captain again when we will reach
New York. I have stopped asking. After all that has happened

on this ship . . . the days of motionless calm, with no wind to move the ship . . . then the terrible storm . . . I am quite content to sit here on deck enjoying the sunshine (which I thought we would never see again) and to make a few notes in my diary. We'll be lucky to reach New York in time for Rosh Ha-Shono.

What will our life be like in the New World? We shall be very poor at first, for I spent all our money to pay the passage on this ship. Theresa and I will miss the great cities of Europe; the art, the music, the wonderful libraries. I shall even miss the little stone snyagogue in Radnitz, with its roof of red clay tiles. Yet I am impatient to reach America. And I know, too, that I would surely have gotten into serious trouble if I had remained in Radnitz as rabbi.

My sermons about the need for change, for reforms in the synagogue, did not please most people. But I know with certainty that Judaism will not stay alive in this modern age unless we *do* make changes in it. We must create a Judaism which our children will understand and want to keep alive. Long before I set out for the New World, I believed in the need for reform. But in the Old World, people think that nothing must change, that things must be done as they have always been done in the past. But—perhaps I was not patient enough? So many of our congregants did not like my ideas. . . .

Then there was my attitude toward the Emperor. I was to give a sermon which was to be a tribute to the Emperor, for his "greatness." But I mentioned him just once, and then went on to what I think are more important matters. Why should I falsely praise a man who would not allow the Jewish people to live as equals with their neighbors? But the government office at Prague sent word that they did not like my sermon, not at all.

But I suppose that the last straw for the government was that I dared to marry young couples without official consent. There is a dreadful law in Bohemia, that no Jews are permitted to marry until another Jew either dies or moves to another province. That is how the Emperor hopes to keep us weak, to keep us from having families. It makes me furious even now to think of such a cruel law. So, I married many Jewish couples who had no government license; I married them according to the laws of God and the customs of our faith, without the permission of the Emperor. And I'm *glad* I did.

No wonder my friends were worried about my safety! I was in trouble with the district rabbi, with the congregation, and with the government. No wonder everyone was relieved when I decided to take my family to America. But I didn't know then that the government would not permit me to leave the country legally, and that Theresa and the baby and I would have to be smuggled out under a load of hay in an oxcart!

But, no matter how, I knew I must go to a free country where I could live as a Jew because it was my right to do so, not because an official of the Emperor decided it was to his advantage to let me live in peace.

The United States is a federal republic where officers of the state serve the people, rather than the people being servants of the state. Men are free to write and speak and worship God in their own way. There are already fifteen thousand Jews in America. Surely many of them believe as

I do. I shall become an American rabbi, and help build a new form of Judaism. Theresa and I will find a new home. Emily will grow up in freedom. How I long to see the shores of America!

SEPTEMBER 15, 1850
Albany, New York

For four years I have been working in Albany as rabbi and teacher, and never in my wildest dreams could I have imagined the events of these past Holy Days!

First, the cantor began to drink again. He had not touched a drop for quite a while—but suddenly, there he was! Despite my warnings.

Then there was the mystery of the missing robe. Who would steal the robe I wear when I lead the services and give my sermons? It has no great value, so I must believe it was stolen just to annoy me.

It wasn't until Spiegel opened his store on Saturday, however, that I began to realize that there was a deliberate plan afoot to embarrass me and to make it impossible for me to continue to lead my congregation. When I reminded Spiegel that all members of the Temple Board had promised me that they would observe the Sabbath, he merely shrugged, indifferently. I was shocked.

But it was not until the next Sabbath that the president of the congregation, Louis Spanier, revealed exactly what he intended to do. As I stood up and was about to begin my sermon, Spanier rose and ordered me not to speak! When, in spite of him, I began, Spanier cried, loudly, "I tell you, you shall not preach today!" And he and his friends walked out of the synagogue! Why does he dislike me so? Is it the changes I have made in the services? Is it the friends I have made for myself and for my people among Gentiles? Is it that I insist on freedom to say what I believe?

But the events which followed were even more shocking. Spanier called the annual meeting of the congregation on a busy weekday afternoon, instead of our usual time, which was the night after Rosh Ha-Shono. He thought my friends would not be there to vote and that he could have me fired. But my friends *were* there, and the meeting went on for eight hours, with neither my friends nor my enemies winning a decision. At last the majority agreed to have me remain as rabbi and ended the meeting. But the president and his little group stayed on and voted me out of office!

I was tempted to resign; to leave the congregation, study law, and open a law office. But I love Judaism too much to turn away from the respect and duty I feel for it. So I went to the synagogue on Rosh Ha-Shono. And, in spite of what happened on that terrible day, I am not sorry.

After the choir had sung, I moved to the ark to take out the Torah, as I had always done. Louis Spanier stepped in front of me. The congregation was very, very still. I moved toward the ark. Spanier would not let me pass. As I moved forward, he struck me, knocking my cap from my head. Then bedlam broke out! Suddenly the congregation was a struggling, shouting mass of fighting people. I felt deeply ashamed when the police came to stop the riot.

When I said, quietly, to Louis Spanier "there is a law to which I can appeal," his reply was as ugly as his behavior. "I have a hundred thousand dollars more than you," he said, insolently. "I do not fear the law! I will ruin you!"

My sadness at this was so great I believe I would have left Albany at once if my friends had not been so loyal. But they resigned from the congregation on the spot, formed a new one, and insisted that I stay on as their rabbi. They rented a third story room in an old building, nailed benches together for pews, and hurried to New York to buy a Torah. Everything was ready for the service by Yom Kippur! I shall never forget how beautiful that service was to me.

I think we shall call the new congregation *Anshe Emeth* —Men of Truth. For my friends are indeed men of truth, ready to give our ancient faith new forms and new life for the world of today and tomorrow.

SUMMER, 1883

Yesterday we made history! The first class to graduate from a Jewish college in the United States! These young men are the very first American-trained rabbis, and they are ready to begin their work. My boys made me very proud yesterday. But I must stop calling them "my boys"—I must get used to calling them "colleagues."

There were seventeen of them when we started, eight years ago, in the drafty basement of the temple. Only four finished and were graduated yesterday. But those four had eight years to study and to decide whether or not they really wished to be rabbis, and that is how it should be.

A class will graduate every year now. These young men will be trained in Jewish knowledge, as well as English speech and American customs, and they will know how to teach Judaism properly to American Jews. A new Jewish faith will arise, full of life and strength, and a blessing to our people.

But we have not always been so successful. Thirty years ago we started Zion College, but it failed, heartbreakingly, because we had no union of congregations to support it. How we worked—but we failed. For over twenty-five years I pleaded, I explained that we Jews must unite for our common good. We almost succeeded at that meeting in Cleveland, so many years ago. But there was too much disagreement among our people. Some were impatient and thought we did not move forward quickly enough. Others, who did not want change, were sure that we moved too fast. And it was impossible for the congregations to agree and to unite.

Even now, though we at last have our Union, it does not include all the congregations, not even all those who share the same beliefs. But we will grow. As our Hebrew Union College graduates begin to reach our people throughout the country, Reform Judaism will grow and become a mighty stream.

And, though it may surprise many people, though our school is modern and American, the basic ideas of Judaism are the heart of our belief. "Judaism is in this very Torah," I told my boys. "A faithful Jew is he whose belief and life are regulated by the Torah to the best of his understanding. There is no Judaism without the Torah."

I explained that we Jews must unite for our common good.

There is still much to do for American Judaism, and much to do for my congregation, my newspaper, my responsibilities to the life of the whole city. And perhaps some day we shall bring all the rabbis together in a great conference, to help one another, to find solutions for the problems that face us all.

Sometimes I feel as though I've only just begun! And I still feel the way I did when, so many years ago, I wrote in the first issue of my newspaper, *The Israelite*:

> Come what may and how it may, I will not swerve a hair's breadth from my convictions. Either I will build up a Judaism suited to the age and breathing the spirit of American freedom, or I will be buried beneath the ruins of the old Judaism. I do not wish to be rich, nor honored, nor recognized, nor beloved; I will do my duty. I will remain true to my convictions.

That's how it was then, and that's just how I feel now. But there is one difference. I'm like the engineer of a train going through a tunnel. As I get near the end, I begin to see light!

What Do You Think?

If you are asked to give the Sermonette at a children's service honoring Rabbi Wise what might you say?

Something for You to Do

Suppose your temple is planning to dedicate one of its stained glass windows to the life of Isaac Mayer Wise. Make a design for such a window.

See the filmstrip *Isaac Mayer Wise: Master Builder of American Judaism*.

You Will Enjoy Reading

"An American Rabbi," *Great Jews Since Bible Times* by ELMA E. LEVINGER, Behrman House, Inc., p. 147.

"The Fight Is On," *The Great March*, Book II, by ROSE G. LURIE, Union of American Hebrew Congregations, p. 162.

"Builders of Judaism," *The Jewish People*, Book III, by DEBORAH PESSIN, United Synagogue of America, p. 216.

"Isaac Mayer Wise: Pioneer of American Judaism," by Rabbi JOSEPH H. GUMBINER, UAHC 1959.

Some More Facts About Isaac Mayer Wise

The father of the Union of American Hebrew Congregations, HUC-JIR, and CCAR, Isaac Mayer Wise was born in Bohemia in 1819, the son of a school teacher. He received his Hebrew education from his grandfather and continued to study in Prague. Isaac was a rabbi in Radnitz only two years and came to the United States in 1846.

Of the many changes he made in his Albany congregations, all were startling for the times. He introduced family pews, sermons in English, a mixed choir, and Confirmation. Wise even counted women in forming a *minyan!*

He broke the custom of each Reform rabbi writing his own prayer book. It was through Wise's efforts that the *Union Prayerbook* was accepted for all congregations to use.

Before Isaac Mayer Wise died in 1900, he added a great new idea to Jewish thought . . . that Judaism should not contain meaningless ceremonies but should be built upon sincere belief in important teachings.

RABBI SOLOMON SCHECHTER
"And the Bush Was Not Consumed"

IT WAS a cold winter night in the little university town of
Cambridge, England. Many of his students would have been
amazed at the angry impatience with which their good professor, Solomon Schechter, marched up and down his study,
past the table where Israel Zangwill and Joseph Jacobs sat
staring at him with an air of amusement. The light from
the lamp fell on a tiny piece of tattered parchment, carefully
covered with glass. Every few minutes the three men paused
in their talk and examined it closely.

"I don't know why you're both being so dense," Schechter
said angrily, his blue-grey eyes blazing behind his glasses.
"You, Joseph, are a student of history. And you, Israel, are a

writer. You, of all people, should understand why I am so excited about this treasure!"

He pointed to the bit of parchment.

"I would stake my reputation as a scholar that it is from the Hebrew text of the book called *The Wisdom of Ben Sirach*. I recognize two of the words and several more letters."

Israel Zangwill pursed his lips in a superior smile.

"You really believe," he drawled, "that those two good ladies, Mrs. Lewis and Mrs. Gibson, have brought you a valuable find? I should hardly consider them scholars, my dear Solomon."

Solomon Schechter seemed about to explode with impatience.

"Israel," he said, pounding on the table, "you know perfectly well that these two ladies do not pretend to be scholars. They were traveling in Egypt and, out of curiosity, bought some pieces of old parchment from a little curio shop. They brought this to me because they thought it might be of interest to me and to Dr. Taylor of Cambridge. They merely brought it to us for an opinion. Dr. Taylor agrees that it is part of a very old Hebrew scroll. I have studied it carefully, and I tell you that it is from the Hebrew text of the book of Ben Sirach, written one hundred years before the Maccabees!"

Joseph Jacobs had been listening intently. His large brown eyes searched his friend's face for a while.

"How can you be so certain, Solomon?" he asked. "The only texts we have ever found of that book are in Greek. The work may have been first written in Hebrew, but the Hebrew text has been lost in antiquity for at least a thousand years.

What makes you think this is from the original Hebrew?"

Schechter stopped his pacing for a moment.

"I *know* it, Jacob. I am positive. If it is found, we will have the oldest Hebrew book known to us except the Bible. But I must prove it. How, how?"

He resumed his pacing.

"I'll tell you how. This piece of parchment and several other very old manuscripts which these ladies brought back with them all came from the same place in Egypt near the city of Cairo. I'm going to Cairo, and I shall search and search until I find the original book. Perhaps I'll find many more old books, or fragments of them. While all of you sit around scoffing and smoking your pipes, *I* am going to Egypt!"

"And," said Zangwill, puffing complacently on his pipe, "what will you do with Matilda and the children while you are chasing old manuscripts all over Egypt?"

"I've already thought of that, my friend," said Schechter, a gleam of triumph in his blue eyes. "The children will stay here in an excellent boarding school. Matilda will come with me. If I find something of value I will bring it back to England where it can be studied by experts. Just wait, my friend! You'll eat your words!"

"Come in, Rabbi." The *shamos* of the Ezra Synagogue in Cairo bowed low from the waist. The pom-pom on his large *yarmelke* shook from side to side as the little man greeted his learned guest.

"We have heard of your work at Cambridge. No doubt you have come to see our exhibits? Here in this case is the Torah scroll written by Ezra himself, after whom our synagogue is named . . ."

116

"Yes, yes," Solomon Schechter interrupted. "This is very interesting to be sure, but—"

"Ah! You want to look at the old books and papers in our *genizah*," the *shamos* said, bobbing up and down. "I know. Come this way, please."

A *genizah* is a burial place for old books. The Jews of ancient times would never destroy a book; when it became too old or worn to be used, the book was buried or hidden away in a secret place, the *genizah*.

Schechter's heart beat faster. He had searched tirelessly through Cairo for his manuscript. Were the doors opening now? What would he find?

The *shamos'* little feet padded softly in their pointed slippers. Schechter followed him, his hat planted firmly on his head, a large leather case clutched under one arm. The *shamos*, pom-pom jiggling with each step, led the way to a dark, narrow staircase.

"Here, Rabbi." He pointed to the steep steps. "The *genizah* is here, up these steps. You will find it dark and dusty. But you are welcome to look around." He shrugged his shoulders. "But there's nothing valuable there."

"Thank you, my friend." Solomon Schechter smiled at the little *shamos*. "You may go about your work. I shall probably be up there most of the day."

He climbed the narrow steps up to the high attic of the synagogue. As the *shamos* had cautioned, it was pitch black and smelled of old books and papers. Over a thousand years of decaying parchment filled the air with dust and ancient odors. Feeling his way in the dark, Dr. Schechter opened his case. He took out a lantern and a large magnifying glass. He lit the lantern and, by its light, saw piles and piles of old books, papers, and parchments heaped about the room helter-skelter.

"Now I understand," he thought, "why these tiny fragments came from Cairo. They never throw anything away! They even hate to bury a Hebrew book. So they just put it up here in the *genizah*. And these old parchments are remarkably well preserved. In most places, they would rot away. But here in Egypt the climate is so dry that the oldest manuscripts still hold together."

Hanging the lantern from a low beam, he moved about the attic, magnifying glass in hand. Carefully, very carefully, so as not to destroy the precious old scraps of scroll, he examined them.

"It is a battlefield of books," he mused, "and the writings of many centuries have shared in the battles. Some are entirely gone, ground to dust by time. Others are squeezed into strange, clumsy shapes. But there is enough material here to keep all the scholars and students in the world busy for many years to come! What a find! Wait till I show some of this to Zangwill and Jacobs!"

Scarcely able to control his excitement, he went down the narrow stairs and asked the little *shamos* if he might pack up the old books and papers and ship them to England for study.

"Of course," the *shamos* shrugged. "I have permission to give you whatever you wish. It is only rubbish up there in the attic."

Schechter smiled. Rubbish! The oldest Hebrew book other than the Bible, the history of the Jews of Egypt, letters from the great Gaonim of Babylonia explaining the Talmud, poems and prayers by some of the greatest men in Jewish history! The scholars in Cambridge would not call this rubbish! He smiled and promised to clean out the attic for the little *shamos*—and that is how he found the great treasure of the Cairo *genizah*.

Scholars worked with Rabbi Schechter for many years, translating the material he had found and putting the ancient manuscripts in order. (Today, after more than fifty years, it has still not all been read.) And, sure enough, among the dusty shreds of parchment, he found most of the Hebrew manuscript written by Ben Sirach hundreds of years ago.

As a result of his scholarship we now know many things about Jewish history we never knew before. Even Israel Zangwill and Joseph Jacobs were forced to admit the importance of the treasures found in that dusty old attic in Cairo.

Some years before, in 1886, a group of Jewish leaders in New York had begun a new school called the Jewish Theological Seminary, in which they trained rabbis especially for congregations in the United States. These leaders knew about the existence of the Hebrew Union College in Cincinnati which trained Reform rabbis, but they were interested in a different kind of school. They felt that Reform Jews had changed the old Jewish customs too much. They loved the Hebrew language and the Jewish people, and they wanted change to come more gradually.

For several years the school made very little progress. A great teacher and leader was needed to build up the new seminary. Dr. Schechter's reputation as a great scholar and a powerful leader had spread through Europe and America. In 1901, Dr. Schechter received a letter.

Dear Rabbi Schechter,

I have the honor of writing to you at the request of a committee of our leaders here in the United States.

Fifteen years ago we opened a new school in New York. We call it the Jewish Theological Seminary. We teach young men to become rabbis for our congregations, which do not want to change the old ways too much.

We seek a scholar and leader to become president of the Seminary. We invite you to accept this position. It will give you the opportunity to influence many hundreds of young men with the ideas of positive Conservative Judaism.

Though we differ in many ways from them, we have the interest and help of many Reform Jewish leaders, including Mr. Louis Marshall and Mr. Jacob Schiff.

Please let us know whether you feel free to accept our offer.

Very sincerely yours,
Mayer Sulzberger

Rabbi Schechter and his wife Matilda discussed the possibility of going to America.

"I don't know if you would be happy there," Matilda worried. "You love Cambridge and London because of their great schools and libraries. All of your friends are here. Life in America will be very different."

The rabbi leaned forward and took Matilda's hand. "You have always thought first of me," he replied. "Always trying to make my life smooth and happy. Everything you have said is true. But still I wish to go to the Seminary in New York.

We need a strong movement for Conservative Judaism in the United States. I am ready to build it. I am ready to go if you are."

That summer the Schechter family bade farewell to their friends and made the long, stormy journey across the Atlantic Ocean to New York City.

For the motto of the Seminary, Rabbi Schechter chose these words from the Bible: "And the bush was not consumed." By this he meant that Jewish life and faith still lived, in spite of the many fires through which the Jewish people had passed.

Rabbi Schechter built the Seminary into a great center of Jewish learning and was its head for the rest of his life. He taught his students to be Conservative Jews, to try to feel themselves a part of *all* the Jewish people, and of the *whole* Jewish tradition, not just the modern and progressive part. He once said, "If a Reform rabbi makes his congregation *give up* Judaism, the institution can be run by a gypsy boy."

However, Rabbi Schechter got along very well with the Reform Jews. He became a close friend of Dr. Kaufmann Kohler, the president of the Hebrew Union College. Both men were great scholars, and together they tried to strengthen Jewish life in America. They did not always agree on how this should be done, but they both wanted the same thing: strong, loyal, American Jews.

In the same year that Solomon Schechter came to America, the Conservative rabbis made their own organization of rabbis, the Rabbinical Assembly of America. Dr. Schechter realized that much of the strength of Reform Judaism came

121

from its national organizations: the college, the conference of rabbis, and the union of congregations. Dr. Schechter believed that the Conservative Jews needed a nation-wide organization of congregations, too.

Solomon Schechter was an impatient man, eager to act. But he knew that a union of Conservative congregations could not succeed until rabbis and other Jews really wanted it enough. He forced himself to postpone his plans. Meanwhile, he went on teaching his students, spreading his ideas to everyone he knew.

At last, it seemed that the time had come to form the national group of which he had dreamed. In February of 1913, Solomon Schechter invited Conservative Jewish leaders to meet with him in New York. He said to them:

> My dear friends, I was born in Roumania, lived in England, and came to the United States to build a living Judaism in the New World. I believe it is time we organize on the basis of positive Judaism. We shall lose our Jews unless we teach them the truth of the Torah, and the need to keep the Sabbath and the rules about kosher food. We must support the Jewish people. We can be Zionists, even if some of us do not want to wear the label. We must teach our children Hebrew and make Hebrew the language of Jewish prayer in America.
>
> Because of the importance of these things, I ask that we form a national body of Conservative congregations.

The audience clapped loud and long. They agreed with Dr. Schechter's ideas; and they created the organization which he wanted. They named it the United Synagogue and elected Rabbi Solomon Schechter its president.

That night Solomon and Matilda sat together in the living room of their home. His great beard was white now, but the blue eyes behind his glasses were still bright and clear. "You see, Matilda," he said, peering over his glasses at his wife, "we were right to come to America. There were no great Jewish libraries . . . we have built one of the greatest at the Seminary. Judaism was weakened . . . we have strengthened it through the growth of the Conservative movement. To the school and the assembly of rabbis we now add the United Synagogue. As my favorite American hero, Abraham Lincoln, said the second time he took office as President of the United States, 'The Almighty has His own Purpose.' Perhaps His purpose for us was that we leave our friends in England and carry on this work in the New World. I'm glad we did and I know you are, too." Matilda did not speak. Neither did Solomon. They didn't have to. Their happiness spoke for them.

What Do You Think?

What did Isaac Mayer Wise and Solomon Schechter have in common?

Something for You to Do

Take a piece of paper and write on it two or three blessings and songs (in Hebrew and/or in English). Then tear the piece of paper into many small pieces, mix them up and throw a few pieces away. Ask a friend or parent to do what Schechter did, to put the scraps of paper together like a picture puzzle and guess what the blessings and songs were.

You Will Enjoy Reading

"The Scholar Who Found Hidden Treasure," *Great Jews Since Bible Times* by ELMA E. LEVINGER, Behrman House, Inc., p. 152.

"The Hidden Treasure," *The Great March*, Book II, by ROSE G. LURIE, Union of American Hebrew Congregations, p. 217.

"Rescued," *Giants on the Earth*, by DEBORAH PESSIN, Behrman House, Inc., p. 89.

"Builders of Judaism," *The Jewish People*, Book III, by DEBORAH PESSIN, United Synagogue of America, p. 222.

Some More Facts About Solomon Schechter

The great scholar, Solomon Schechter, was born in Roumania in 1847. His father gave him a rabbinical education. Then young Solomon decided to study in Vienna. Even after he became a rabbi, he went to Berlin to continue his studies under the great German Talmudists.

So great did Solomon's reputation as a scholar grow that Claude Montefiore asked him to come to England to be his private teacher. Solomon knew no English when he arrived. He learned the language so well that his writings were considered great gifts to English literature. He was even appointed a professor at Cambridge University.

His many writings gave a clear explanation of what Jews believed.

He died in New York City in 1915, after bringing his great knowledge to serve American Jewry and the Conservative movement.

EMMA LAZARUS
"Give Me Your Tired, Your Poor . . ."

THE narrow four-story house in which the Lazarus family lived was very much like the other houses on West Fourteenth Street. And all the seven Lazarus children were very much like most other Jewish children in New York City in the middle of the nineteenth century. All of them, that is, but little Emma Lazarus.

Even as a small girl, Emma was different. Her parents, Moses and Hettie, sensed it from the very beginning. Moses spent a great deal of time with his family. He soon found that, of all his children, it was little Emma whose company he most enjoyed. He was delighted with her endless curiosity and quick understanding. For hours at a time he answered her questions and discussed the ideas that darted in and out of her eager mind.

Emma was frailer than the other children. She did not play and run outside as the others did, but spent hours quietly in the house, content with her books and her thoughts. Public school was too taxing for her frail little body; she had her lessons at home with a private teacher. The tutor was a shy young man; but before he knew it, he found himself talking easily to Emma and sharing with her his enthusiasm for the new books they read together.

As Emma grew up, books became a more and more important part of her life. Often her father would find her in her room, her blue-grey eyes intent on the volume of English poems before her. She was a charming little figure, with her brown hair brushed back from her thin face and tied with a big ribbon, as she sat with her nose buried in a book, almost lost to the world.

But as far as religion was concerned, Emma only knew that her family was Jewish because they belonged to a synagogue and because they would have a Seder at Passover time, but not much more. For the most part, her world was her family and her books, mostly English poetry.

"Father," said Emma one day as they sat chatting together, "where did our family come from before we were Americans?"

"Portugal," he answered. "Why do you ask, Emma?"

"I have been studying American history," she said, her thin little face serious and intent. "I've discovered that all Americans except the Indians came here from some other country. Why did our people leave Portugal?"

"For just the same reason that Jews left Spain in the

fifteenth and sixteenth centuries. They were treated dreadfully and were finally forced to choose either to become Christians or to leave the country. Those who left wandered for many years searching for a home. Some Jews settled in America even before the Revolutionary War. Your great-grandfather was among them."

Emma's forehead wrinkled in a deep frown.

"But now that we are safe here, we don't have to worry about such things, do we?"

Her father smiled fondly and patted her head.

"No, my dear, we don't have to worry about such things."

The years slipped by quietly in the Lazarus household. Emma knew that there was a Civil War because some of her cousins fought in the Grand Army of the Republic, but for the most part life was calm and uneventful.

By the time she was sixteen, Emma had begun to put her thoughts and feelings into poetry. At first she thought the verses were not very good and was too shy to show them to anyone. But she continued to write. At last, she gathered up all her courage and showed the carefully written poems to her father. He read them at once.

"Why, Emma," he said, proudly, when he had finished, "these are very fine. You are a real poet. Perhaps we should publish your poems in a book."

This was more than Emma had dared hope.

"Oh, Father, do you really think they are good enough?" Her eyes danced with excitement. "Because if you really think so, I should love to have a book published! It would make me so happy!"

A few days after this conversation Emma met the great

127

writer, Ralph Waldo Emerson, at the home of old friends. Emma had read most of his books and was thrilled when her host introduced her to the tall, grey-haired poet with the kindly eyes. Encouraged by his interest in her, Emma shyly told Emerson that she hoped soon to publish her first book of poems. He asked her to send a copy of her book to his home in Concord. Emma went home that night happier than she had ever been before.

In time Emma became well known for her own poems and for her translations of books written in other languages. She often wrote to Emerson and he always answered with suggestions for improving her writing and with warm praise for her work.

But the life of a writer has its disappointments as well as its joys. For, some years later, Emerson published a large collection of what he thought were the greatest poems ever written in the English language. Emma immediately bought the book and eagerly searched the list of poets. Not *one* of her own poems was included. Heartbroken, Emma wept bitterly. Why had Emerson praised her work all these years and not put even one of her poems in his collection? Emma did not understand. She was so unhappy that she became ill. But, though they continued to write to each other, Emma never mentioned a word of her deep disappointment to Emerson.

One day a letter came for Emma postmarked "Concord, Mass." She opened it eagerly. It was an invitation to visit the Emersons.

As Emma stepped out of the train at the Concord station, she saw Emerson's tall, thin figure, waiting patiently on the platform. He greeted her warmly and carried her suitcase to the waiting wagon.

The Emersons lived in a large square grey house, fenced by white pickets and shaded by tall trees. Emma had a wonderful time in Concord. She discussed books and writing with Emerson and his friend, William Ellery Channing. She visited the house where Thoreau had lived. But through all the happy time of her visit, she was not able to bring herself to ask Emerson why her work had not been included in his anthology of poems.

During her early years, Emma had given little thought to being Jewish. Of course, she was proud to be heir to the great history of the Jews. She had translated some of the early Spanish-Jewish poets, among them the work of Yehudah Halevi. She had even written a poem about a synagogue at Newport, the very first Jewish house of worship in the United States. But Emma really thought of herself as a part of the great world. Being Jewish seemed a small, unimportant part of her life.

When Emma was a young woman in her thirties, Rabbi Gottheil of Temple Emanu-El in New York asked her to help him prepare a new edition of the prayer book, for he knew her talent as a writer would make the book a beautiful one. He was rather shocked when Emma said: "I am a poet —I do not write to order. I will gladly assist you as far as I can, but that will not be much. I shall always be loyal to my people, but I feel no religious fervor in my soul. . . ."

But events in far-off Russia were to change her attitude. In May of 1881, enraged mobs murderously attacked the overcrowded Jewish communities in the Pale of Settlement. Thousands of Jews were killed. Thousands more were wounded or driven from their homes. Jewish property was stolen. Jewish homes were burned. The cruel tyranny of the Czar's government increased daily. The Russian government passed new laws making life even more unbearable for the Jews.

Hundreds of thousands of poor Jews fled from Russia with little more than what they could carry with them. They set out to find new homes in the West, particularly in America. The first refugees arrived in New York in August, 1881. Penniless, homeless, they were unloaded at Ward's Island in upper Manhattan. They had been packed like animals in the cattle section of the ship. Flimsy huts were built as temporary houses for them. They had to be fed. The sick must be cared for. Lawyers were needed to solve the legal problems resulting from their entry into the United States. A committee was hastily formed to help meet the emergency.

Emma went to Ward's Island to see the refugees. With a feeling of great pain and shock she saw European Jews for the first time. Bearded men, dressed in long black coats and wide-brimmed hats, cried out in a strange language. Women in shawls and peasant skirts clutched sobbing babies to their breasts and swayed from side to side, trying to quiet them. Everyone was hungry, thirsty and tired. Many were sick. These were the Jews. In her heart, Emma recognized them as her own people.

At that moment, Emma's life as a Jew was changed forever. She joined the committee to solve the problems of these immigrants. On the night of February 1, 1882, there was a

With a feeling of great pain and shock she saw European
Jews for the first time.

mass meeting in Chittering Hall. The hall was crowded with people eager to help. Many of the city's leading Christians were there, as well as Jewish leaders. Emma had been asked to speak but she had always lived such a quiet life that she felt unable to face so many people. Instead, she had written a poem called "The Banner of the Jew."

The crowd grew quiet as the chairman announced that he would read a poem by the well-known poetess, Emma Lazarus—a poem written especially for the occasion. These are a few of Emma's lines.

> Let but an Ezra rise anew,
> To lift the Banner of the Jew!
>
> "A rag, a mock at first . . . ere long,
> When men have bled and women wept,
> To guard its precious folds from wrong,
> Even they who shrank, even they who slept,
> Shall leap to bless it, and to save.
> Strike! for the brave revere the brave!"

When he had finished, there was silence. Then the crowd applauded wildly.

The life and writing of Emma Lazarus changed completely. She learned Hebrew. She helped with the prayers and translations as Rabbi Gottheil had asked. She wrote many letters about the possibility of rebuilding Jewish life in Palestine. She helped settle Russian Jews in the United States, and she wrote many poems on Jewish themes.

One of her best-known poems, "Gifts," tells of the desires of the great nations of history. The Egyptian wanted wealth, the Greek desired beauty, and the Roman asked for power. Each nation received its wish, and then disappeared from history. The Jew asked for truth. And because the Jew sought truth, his people lives on from age to age. In the last part of the poem, Emma wrote:

O Godhead, give me Truth! the Hebrew cried
His prayer was granted; he became a slave
Of the idea, the pilgrim far and wide,
Cursed, hated, and scourged with none to save.
The Pharaohs knew him, and when Greece beheld,
His wisdom wore the hoary crown of Eld.
Beauty he hath forsworn, and wealth and power.
Seek him today, and find in every land.
No fire consumes him, neither floods devour;
Immortal through the lamp within his hand.

About two years later, Emma had just returned from a trip to Europe when she received a visit from an old friend, William M. Evarts, former Secretary of State of the United States. In his striped trousers and dark coat, Evarts looked every inch the diplomat.

Evarts brought exciting news. "Emma, perhaps you heard in Europe that France is preparing a remarkable gift to America? It is an enormous statue to be called 'Liberty,' or 'Liberty Enlightening the World.' It will stand on Bedloe's Island."

"In New York harbor?" Emma exclaimed. "Every immigrant to the United States will see it as his ship comes in!"

"Exactly," Evarts replied. "All over the world the poor and homeless will think of liberty when they see it. I thought you would like to help with the project."

"But, William," Emma said, puzzled, "what can I do?"

"We need money. A huge foundation must be built on the island upon which the statue will stand. We are going to hold an auction in the gallery at Fourth Avenue and Twenty-third Street. We shall sell compositions written in their own hand by famous writers like Longfellow, Walt Whitman, Bret Harte, and Mark Twain. The money paid for these manuscripts will go into a fund to build the foundation and the pedestal for the Statue of Liberty. Will you give us a poem for the auction?"

Emma thought for a moment. "You know that this is hard for me to do," Emma said slowly. "I have to be free to write as I feel."

"I know that, Emma."

"But I wish to help my people, the Jews. I also wish to help *all* men driven by oppressors to seek a new home in a strange land. The thought of America as a home for the unwanted and oppressed is close to my heart. I shall try to write something for the auction."

When William Evarts left, Emma sat down at her desk. "A huge Statue of Liberty," she thought, "at the entrance of New York harbor—to welcome the poor and the homeless whom no one else wants."

For a long time she sat, her forehead resting on her hand. At last she took up her pen and began to write these words:

The New Colossus

Not like the brazen giant of Greek fame,
With conquering limbs astride from land to land;
Here at our sea-washed, sunset gates shall stand
A mighty woman with a torch, whose flame
Is the imprisoned lightning, and her name
Mother of Exiles. From her beacon-hand
Glows worldwide welcome, her mild eyes command
The air-bridged harbor that twin cities frame.

'Keep, ancient lands, your storied pomp!' cries she
With silent lips. 'Give me your tired, your poor,
Your huddled masses yearning to breathe free,
The wretched refuse of your teeming shore.
Send these, the homeless, tempest-tost to me.
I lift my lamp beside the golden door!'

The auction raised thousands of dollars. Emma's poem sold for fifteen hundred dollars! All the money went to build the pedestal for the statue.

The following year the Statue of Liberty was set in its place on Bedloe's Island. To millions of new Americans it has been their first sight of America, and to people from all over the world it means freedom and hope.

In the year 1903, several years after the death of Emma Lazarus, her poem was cast in bronze and placed permanently at the base of the Statue of Liberty. There you may see it to this very day.

What Do You Think?

Why was the poem "The New Colossus," written by Emma Lazarus, so appropriate for the Statue of Liberty?

Something for You to Do

Try to write some rhymes about Emma Lazarus to the tune of "Dayenu." For example:
—If Emma had been only a good Jewish girl
              and not a poet   Dayenu
—If Emma had been only a great poet
              but had not. . . .

Have a poetry contest to see who can write a Jewish poem the class likes best.

Listen to a record of "The Golden Door," Irving Berlin's song to Emma's words.

You Will Enjoy Reading

"Of Thee I Sing," *The Great March*, Book II, by ROSE G. LURIE, Union of American Hebrew Congregations, p. 179.

"Emma Lazarus, Poet of Her People," *Great Jewish Women*, by ELMA EHRLICH LEVINGER, Behrman House, Inc., p. 140.

"Emma Lazarus Comes Home Again," *Giants on the Earth*, by DEBORAH PESSIN, Behrman House, Inc., p. 9.

Some More Facts About Emma Lazarus

Emma Lazarus was born in New York City in 1849. Her first volume of poetry was published in 1867. Emma's way of writing resembled the poetry of ancient Greece.

In her early years she disliked Jewish things. But she was friendly with many poets. One of them, Edmund Stedman, scolded her for lack of interest in her Jewish heritage. Another, John Burroughs, told her of the influence of Judaism in the works of the great writers, Walt Whitman and Thomas Carlyle.

Just after her visit to Ward's Island (as in the story), Emma read an article in *Century Magazine* which defended the Russian Czar's persecution of the Jews. Emma wrote a fiery reply telling how wrong such cruelty was. Almost overnight she had become a crusader for the Jews.

Emma learned Hebrew. She translated many old Jewish poems into English, so that many would be able to enjoy their beauty.

When Emma Lazarus died in 1887, she knew that the thousands of Jewish immigrants were her friends.

ELIEZER BEN YEHUDAH
Father of a Language

I knew Eliezer ben Yehudah for forty years. I became acquainted with him when he first came to Palestine. Now that I am getting old (*zaken*, as Eliezer would say, because he would speak only Hebrew), I had better write down some of the things I remember about him before I forget.

I feel a need to write about Eliezer because if I don't, who will? We all owe him a great deal. If it had not been for Eliezer, the Jews here in Palestine would never have begun to write and speak in Hebrew. We owe our *safah b'rurah*, our pure Hebrew speech, to him. He was a man who was so concerned with one idea that often he seemed rude and difficult and very few people liked him, but they did not understand the importance of what he was trying to do. That is why I must leave these notes behind. For when people speak Hebrew in future years, they should know how hard Eliezer worked to make it possible.

Of course, Hebrew was never really a dead language. Our people always prayed in Hebrew. They wrote and studied books in Hebrew. But these were always religious books and were apart from everyday life. Children never spoke Hebrew when they played together. Women did not speak to shopkeepers in Hebrew. That is why, when Eliezer ben Yehudah began to use Hebrew for everyday purposes, the pious men became angry. They thought Hebrew was only for prayer and study, not for games or conversation or ordinary things.

But I am rambling on, getting ahead of my story. I guess that's what happens when you become *zaken*. Now, let me see . . . oh, yes. Eliezer once told me how it all began. He was born in Lushki, a small town near Vilna. That means that he was a *Litvak*, a Lithuanian, although I am sure that Eliezer would have been angry if I called him a Litvak. He wanted to be known only as an *Ivri*, a Hebrew. But he was a *Litvak*, whether he liked it or not. And everyone knows how strong-willed the Litvaks are! Which may account for Eliezer's stubbornness about his big idea.

He once told me about his studies with his teacher, Rabbi Joseph Bloker. As a boy, Eliezer had studied all the usual Jewish books—the Bible with Rashi, the Talmud, and the later codes of Jewish law. But when he studied with Rabbi Bloker, things were different. Bloker was a *maskil*, one who believed that Jews should know general history and science and all the other subjects as well as Jewish studies. He also

138

believed that these other things should be taught in Hebrew.

The result was that he taught Eliezer traditional Talmud and Jewish law codes during the day, but at night he introduced him to a very different kind of book, also written in Hebrew. At first, when Eliezer told me this, I could hardly believe it! At night the rabbi and his student read *Robinson Crusoe* in Hebrew! Imagine! (I wonder what the servant, Friday, was called in Hebrew. Was it *Yom hashishi* or *Erev Shabbat*?)

Anyhow, because of this boyhood experience, Eliezer believed that Hebrew should be used for everyday speech. That's why he changed his name from Eliezer Perlman to Eliezer ben Yehudah. Yehudah was his father's Hebrew name. And nothing would do except that Eliezer be known as Eliezer ben Yehudah.

After he left the yeshivah, he thought he would study to be a doctor. He soon changed his mind about that and became a teacher instead. I think it was at this time he decided to go to Palestine, because after some years of study in Paris, he prepared to set off.

I think it was in 1882 that Eliezer went to Palestine, by way of Vienna, where he married Deborah. She had taught him Russian during the old days in Lithuania. It was the kind of marriage that we say was made in heaven. But there was one thing Deborah was not prepared for. On the ship to Palestine, Eliezer and Deborah had a very serious talk. "Deborah," he said to her, "I want you to promise that once we arrive in Palestine we speak *only* in Hebrew. My purpose in life is to revive the Hebrew language. Someone has to start by *speaking* Hebrew. I want our family to be the first."

"But Eliezer," she said, helplessly, "I know very little Hebrew. How can I speak only Hebrew?"

"During the voyage, while we have time, I will begin to teach you. Listen. You know the word *shalom*?"

"Yes, Eliezer. Shalom means peace."

"Right! So it does. But it is also a greeting. So let us say that shalom means hello and good-bye as well as peace. Now, *shalom*, Deborah. What do you say to me?"

"Shalom, Eliezer."

That's how they started. By the time the ship arrived in Haifa, Deborah knew quite a bit. When their first child arrived, a boy whom they named Ittamar, Deborah could speak to the baby in simple Hebrew words.

Eliezer was not a strong man physically and Deborah was rather frail, too. They both had to fight the dread disease tuberculosis. That is probably why Eliezer was always very thin. After Ittamar was born, I suggested that Eliezer hire a part-time maid to help Deborah. They had very little money, but I felt that some help was badly needed in their home. Eliezer said *todah*, "thank you," for the suggestion and promised he would talk it over with Deborah.

By then, I was one of the few people in Palestine who could understand him and talk with him. His strange ideas of reviving Hebrew appealed to me. However, I had my doubts; I had never heard of any other language being brought back to life so many centuries after it was no longer spoken.

Eliezer and Deborah discussed hiring someone to help around the house. But they decided against it because, as Eliezer explained to me, the maid would not know how to speak Hebrew. They had sworn that Ittamar would hear only the *safah b'rurah*. The result was . . . no maid. They did all the work themselves. *That's* how determined Eliezer was.

For three years, little Ittamar did not speak one single word. Neighbors and friends were angry at Eliezer and Deborah and said that the boy did not speak because he heard only his mother and father talking to him in Hebrew. Other children had playmates who spoke Russian or German or English. They said that Ittamar would never learn to talk if this continued.

One day I went to visit Eliezer. I found him sitting on the floor with Ittamar, a bright-looking little boy, standing before him like a tiny soldier. "Look, look," Eliezer called to me, in Hebrew, "watch this!"

He said to Ittamar: *"Sim etsbah al rosh."* (Put your finger on your head.) Ittamar obeyed at once, putting his pudgy index finger on top of his thick, curly hair.

"Sim etsbah al ozen," his father said. Ittamar moved his little finger from his head to his ear.

"Al peh!" came the command. Ittamar placed his finger against his mouth. *"Yeled tov, yeled tov! Zeh nachon!"* (Good boy, good boy! That's correct!) Eliezer said smiling. He hugged Ittamar and gave him a piece of candy.

"You see," he said proudly, "Ittamar knows all the words other children know at his age. Soon he will speak and, for the first time since the days of the Bible, a Jewish child's first words will be in Hebrew."

My friend Eliezer was right. Ittamar soon spoke well. When he was older his mother would send him to the store for *lechem, chalav* or *basar.* At first it was very hard for the storekeeper to understand but somehow little Ittamar always came home with the bread or milk or meat his mother had sent him for.

Ittamar began to make friends. After a while his playmates enjoyed learning the Hebrew words for things. They would play *kadur* (ball) on the playground. Soon the sound of boys and girls calling out in Hebrew as they played their games was familiar in the neighborhood where the ben Yehudahs lived.

In those days the Turks ruled Palestine. Turkey was called "the sick man of Europe," for the Turkish government in Palestine did not run things well. If you wanted anything done, you had to bribe an official. Eliezer had no trouble at all in unearthing the Hebrew word for bribe. It was right in the Bible, the word *shohad*. He spoke his mind quite fearlessly. He made passionate speeches against the government, which he called *memshelet hashohad*, the government of bribes. He did not conceal his belief that the Jews in Palestine should be free to rule themselves. He told everyone that the Jewish people would have a great and free future based on the homeland in Palestine, and the Jews would come there to live and speak the Hebrew language, *Ivrit*.

One night there was a loud pounding on the door. The ben Yehudah family woke up with a start. Eliezer threw a coat over his shoulders and shuffled to the door. He cautiously opened the door a crack, only to have it forced open wide by a Turkish policeman.

"You are under arrest," the policeman said in a harsh voice, "for teaching the Jews to revolt against the government!"

And even in this situation, Eliezer spoke Hebrew: *"Ani naki, ani naki!"* (I am innocent, I am innocent!)

But the policeman did not understand Hebrew. He barely gave Eliezer time to put on his clothes, then seized him by the arm, ready to march him off to prison.

"B'vakashah, bakai rega echad," Eliezer pleaded. (Please wait one minute.) He kissed Deborah and Ittamar and hurriedly picked up some papers and notebooks. Then he was ready to go.

He had grabbed the papers and notebooks because in that moment he had thought of a way to use his time while in prison, and it was there he began his great work, a dictionary of the Hebrew language.

Since people had not spoken everyday Hebrew for so long, many of the words needed for new things did not exist. Eliezer began to invent them. Sometimes he took a Hebrew word and changed it a little to give it a new meaning. Sometimes he borrowed words from other languages and put them in Hebrew form. He intended to write all these words down so that every word needed for everyday speech could be found in the Hebrew language.

Eliezer began this work in the Turkish prison. He continued it long after the police released him. Right at the start, he needed a word for "dictionary." There was no such word in the Hebrew language. But there was a Hebrew word for "word"—*millah*. He changed it just a little and called his dictionary a *millon*.

When he needed a word for something modern like "telephone," he borrowed from another language and put it in Hebrew letters and grammar. In this way, "telephone" became *telefon* and "to telephone," *letalpain*. Whenever he found or made up a Hebrew word, Eliezer wrote it down in his *millon*.

Since there were very few Hebrew books in Palestine in those days, Eliezer began to travel to the great libraries of Paris, Berlin, Rome, London and New York. Wherever he went, he took along his notebooks. Year after year, the *millon* grew until, at last, it became as thick as the largest dictionaries you see in libraries. When it was finished it filled sixteen books!

What had started as a strange hobby became a very important work. Everytime I hear children in the State of Israel speaking Hebrew as their daily language, I think of my friend Eliezer. I remember how stubborn he was and how hard he worked. I also think of Deborah and what a hard life she had.

I am very glad that I have been able to write down these things I remember about my friend Eliezer. I do not mean to say that he alone was responsible for reviving the Hebrew language, but without his stubbornness and determination, it might not have happened as it did. Others joined with him. There was soon a little circle of us who agreed that the new life of the Jewish people in Palestine should include new life for our ancient language. And as the years went by, more and more people spoke and wrote Hebrew. Today it is the everyday language of the State of Israel. And we cannot publish enough books in Hebrew to satisfy our readers. We have dozens of newspapers, all in Hebrew. And the one man who did the most to bring Hebrew back to life was Eliezer ben Yehudah, the stubborn Palestinian Litvak.

What Do You Think?

If the pious men had succeeded in their wish and Hebrew had remained only a language of prayer, what language would be used in Israel today?

Something for You to Do

Pretend you have to prepare a Hebrew dictionary at the time of Eliezer ben Yehudah. Make a list of words you might have to make up. If possible, check a real Hebrew dictionary and see if your words are included and what they are in Hebrew.

See the filmstrip *Eliezer ben Yehuda,* Jewish Agency for Israel.

You Will Enjoy Reading

"Lost! A Hundred Dollars," *The Great March,* Book II, by ROSE G. LURIE, Union of American Hebrew Congregations, p. 190.

Some More Facts About Eliezer ben Yehudah

Eliezer ben Yehudah was born in 1857. When he studied modern Hebrew grammar under Rabbi Joseph Bloker, all classes had to be held in secrecy. Such learning was forbidden by the strict rules of Lithuanian Jewry.

In 1879 ben Yehudah entered a medical school in Paris. But he contracted tuberculosis and left for the warmer climate of Algeria. Here he wrote articles for a Palestinian Hebrew magazine.

Two years later he settled in Eretz Yisroel and became an editor. Ben Yehudah founded his own magazine, *Hats'vi,* (The Deer) in order to spread his idea of bringing back Hebrew as a spoken language. He became a leader in the Pure Language Society, and ben Yehudah's idea soon became a powerful force in the country.

Before Eliezer ben Yehudah died in 1922, he saw the founding of Israel's first daily Hebrew newspaper, *Doar Hayom* (The Daily Mail), another product of his work. He also put together a 16-volume Hebrew dictionary. Most important, he saw Hebrew return as Israel's spoken language.

14

HENRIETTA SZOLD
"The Healing of the Daughter of My People"

OCTOBER 22, 1903
New York City

Dear Bertha:

In class today I suddenly realized that I am the only woman student among all the men at the Jewish Theological Seminary. It feels a little odd, goodness knows, to go back to school at the age of 43—but to be the only woman at a rabbinical seminary—that is really a strange feeling! But the rabbinical students and teachers are all very nice to me. They remember Father with great respect as a devoted scholar and rabbi. I know that, though in my girlhood women were not welcome in colleges and universities, what he taught me—history, Hebrew, languages, great books—has made it possible for me to study side by side with these learned men and not feel too ignorant. But still they don't quite know what to make of a woman student, especially in the class in Talmud!

But I don't mind difficult new tasks. Remember the school we started at home in Baltimore for the refugee Jews who had just come from Czarist Russia? I remember the surprise on the faces of the ladies in our Literary Society when I suggested a night school where these poor people could learn English. Who'd ever heard of a *night* school before? And some of the ladies turned up their noses at the poor Jews from Eastern Europe. Others didn't mind giving money but preferred that someone else do the actual work. But, happily, most of them understood what I meant when I told them to work *with* the new people, not *for* them. And it really worked out wonderfully. We finally had several hundred students in our night classes, learning all kinds of useful subjects—English, arithmetic, bookkeeping, Hebrew—and even dressmaking!

Do you know what I remember best about our school? Our students! After we had scrubbed and swept and painted the old store we rented, and our few blackboards and books were in place—our students began to arrive. The thrill of seeing old men with grey beards sitting in class next to young boys! They all wanted to learn English. And the old people were not ashamed to study, sitting right next to their children and grandchildren. No one was too proud or too shy to learn. So I must not be ashamed of my ignorance, nor of being the only woman among these young men half my age.

147

Sometimes, Bertha, I feel discouraged about how little American Jews know of their own Jewish tradition. It is such a wonderful one. Sometimes it seems as though all those years of hard work with the Jewish Publication Society in Philadelphia were just a drop in the bucket. Remember how you used to tease me for bringing my work home with me at night? But I could not rest—there was so much to be done and hardly anyone to do it. We still need hundreds more good books about Judaism. But I am not really discouraged. We made a beginning and this is what matters.

Bertha, in the past year I have met many new people and heard much discussion of many new, perhaps startling ideas. I know that many of our cautious friends may laugh at me and think me a dreamer, but I have become a Zionist. Since the Jews were expelled from Palestine two thousand years ago, they have never had a land of their own. They have been scattered throughout the world. They have been mistreated and driven from one place to another. Zionism is working to build a home in Palestine for our people. I want to help with that work. It is too soon to tell what Zionists may be able to accomplish. But one thing is clear—Zionism can give our sad and weary people a new hope, an ideal to work for, a dream that may come true. Someday, perhaps I can go to Palestine and see with my own eyes what the *chalutsim*, our brave Jewish pioneers, are building there.

I know you, Bertha, and I can almost hear you saying: "If you loved your work with the Russian Jews so much, why did you leave? And if you thought the work of the Jewish Publication Society was so important, why have you gone to New York to study?"

But, Bertha, everything I have done in my life is part of

one thing. It is learning I have been seeking—sometimes learning for others, sometimes for myself. Our people have always treasured learning—we are, after all, the People of the Book.

But I want to help others too. What matters the most to people before they can really learn with open minds and untroubled hearts is help—practical help, help for living, the kind of help we gave the Russian Jews in our night school.

Dear Bertha, I am so busy and cannot write as often as I would like to. Please share this letter with the family. Write soon.

Your loving sister,
Henrietta

FEBRUARY 25, 1912
New York City

Dear Bertha:-

Today has been one of the most exciting days of my life! I know that you have been worried about my health, especially since I returned from my trip to Palestine. But Bertha, today, though I am in my fifties, old enough to be a grandmother, I felt such happiness, such a feeling of joy in my work and hope for the future that the years mean nothing to me.

Do you remember the terrible things I told you I had seen in Palestine? The children blinded by trachoma, the hundreds of people sick and dying of malaria, the poverty and ignorance and filth? The diseased, uncared-for Arabs and Jews without doctors or hospitals to care for them? And the sadness of wanting to help them and not knowing what to do?

Well, today we did it! Yesterday I met with the small group of Jewish women who are members of my Study Circle. Before the meeting a few of us had met and had agreed upon a plan. I am afraid I shocked the group a little when I began the meeting by saying:

"The members of this Study Circle are very good at drinking tea and reading papers. That is why serious Zionists look upon us as organizers of strawberry festivals."

They really looked quite upset. I went on:

"We have wasted enough time with this foolishness, this talk and tea drinking! Let's get to the practical work for Palestine. We women are supposed to care for the health of our families. Why don't we try to improve the health of our people in Palestine? We can send nurses and medicines. In time we can support medical and health programs for the whole country. There is no end to what we can do if we try."

"But this will take large sums of money," one woman protested.

"Of course it will! That is why we must start at once! Raising this money is the most important thing we can do now. And we will succeed! There will be no counting the rewards in health and happiness for our people in Palestine!"

Well, you can imagine the effect of *that*. Some of the women objected; they thought it too big a job for us. But my friends (and especially those who had been to Palestine themselves) stood behind me. At last, after hours of discussion, thirty-eight women agreed to form the first chapter of a group which will improve public health and send medical help to Palestine. We plan to start by sending two nurses to visit and treat the sick.

This was our first meeting and it was Purim. So we named our organization "Hadassah." This is the Hebrew name of Queen Esther, and it also means "myrtle." For our motto we chose the words of the prophet Jeremiah: "The healing of the daughter of my people."

And we shall heal our people in Zion! I'm too excited to write any more.

Love,
Henrietta

NOVEMBER 11, 1918
New York City

Dear Bertha:

At last the terrible war is over! For four long years we have prayed for peace; at last it is here. Now we can turn our hands and hearts to the tasks of peace.

Last July 25th, our first American Zionist Medical Unit left for Palestine. It has taken Hadassah six years to accomplish this, but at last! Think of it! Forty-four people—doctors, nurses and public health experts—sailed that day. In the hold of the ship was enough equipment for a fifty-bed hospital. The workers waved from the deck, the band played, steam whistles blew as the ship left the pier. Now that the world is at peace, our work of healing can go on in Palestine.

All of New York has gone mad with joy at the end of the war. Our Hadassah office was in an uproar. When we heard the shouts of joy and the ringing of the bells all two hundred of us rushed into the main office. The girls were crying, dancing, jumping up and down with joy. But Rabbi Kohn calmed them. He spoke to us quietly on the meaning of peace. Tears streamed down his cheeks.

Then we closed the office and I lost myself in the crowd which surged along Fifth Avenue. Among the marching people was a Zionist group singing *Hatikvah*. They carried an American flag and a large picture of Theodor Herzl. An old bearded Jew, who reminded me of the Russian Jews in our school in Baltimore so many years ago, walked beside me. In front of him a young girl marched carrying a small blue and white Zionist flag. The old man touched her on the shoulder and said in Yiddish: "Please let me carry the flag only a little while."

There I was, Bertha, crying right in the middle of Fifth Avenue! But they were tears of joy, the kind you shed at a wedding. There is peace—no more war, ever. And we Jews have a homeland in Palestine. And, at this very moment in the Holy Land, our Hadassah workers are helping to heal the sick. "My cup runneth over."

With love,
Henrietta

September 21, 1941
Jerusalem, Palestine

Dear Bertha:

Once more it is the eve of Rosh Ha-shono. And still another year begins with war—World War II. It is two years since the war began—will it ever end? I feel my eighty-one years, Bertha. But it seems as though there is no time to allow myself to grow old. There is still so much to do that I cannot hope to rest.

The most important thing in life to me now is Youth Aliyah. Hadassah formed it in 1934 when we knew that we must save the children from the Nazi countries and bring them safely to our homeland in Palestine. Seven or eight years ago I was about to return to America. At last, I thought, it is time to rest. But Adolf Hitler changed my mind. When that monster became dictator of Germany, I knew I must stay in Palestine and try to save as many people as we could rescue. Youth Aliyah takes all my time and strength. We must save the children!

I always go to the dock at Haifa to meet the ships as they come in. There were forty-three boys and girls in the first group that arrived several years ago. They were bright-eyed children, lonesome for home perhaps, but excited about their trip to a new land. I went with them to Ain Harod. The older settlers were wonderful to them. They did everything they could to welcome the young people to the *K'vutzah*. Soon the young immigrants felt at home.

But not all the children have been so lucky. Year after year, I have noticed a change. The longer they lived under the Nazis, the more they became sick, bitter, without hope for the future. They did not trust anyone, because in Germany every hand had been against them. It took weeks and months of patient effort for our social workers and doctors to win their trust.

Eight thousand children have arrived so far. Do you realize what that means, Bertha? Eight thousand young people have been saved and will have a chance for freedom and a happy life in Palestine. Thank God for the life-saving work of Hadassah!

You know the Arabs are using violence and terror to stop us. They even killed two Hadassah nurses on their way to take care of *Arab* patients. I spoke to the High Commissioner about these terrible acts, reminding him of his responsibility to secure peace and prosperity in the Holy Land. But we too have responsibilities. I also warned our young people to use self-control wherever there is a clash between Jews and Arabs.

We hope for friendship with our Arab neighbors. We want to develop the country for the good of both the Jews and the Arabs. We hope that the Arabs will come to understand this and work with us. We do not know what the future will bring, but we pray and work for healing and peace.

Others will carry on the work I began so long ago. Little Hadassah has grown into the largest Jewish organization in the world. We have 300,000 members in all the cities of the United States. Our loyal women work tirelessly to build hospitals, train nurses, send medical supplies and support a big health program in Palestine.

I must prepare to go to the synagogue now. May you and all our dear ones have a happy and blessed New Year.

Your loving sister,
Henrietta

What Do You Think?

Henrietta Szold has often been called a mother of Israel. Why?

Something for You to Do

Write a letter to someone in a Youth Aliyah Village and ask where they were born, how and when they came to Israel, what they do now and what they hope to do when they grow up. (Send your letter c/o Hadassah 65 E. 52nd St., New York City, N. Y. 10022.)

You Will Enjoy Reading

"Mother of Palestine," *They Fought for Freedom*, by ELMA E. LEVINGER, Union of American Hebrew Congregations.

Meier Shfeya: A Children's Village in Israel, by SONIA GIDAL, Behrman House, Inc.

Great Jewish Women by ELMA E. LEVINGER, Behrman House, Inc.

Some More Facts About Henrietta Szold

Henrietta Szold was born in 1860 into an intensely Jewish family. Her father, a brilliant rabbi, taught her a reverence for learning and a love for people.

After graduating high school Henrietta became a teacher. She also wrote articles for Jewish magazines under the pen-name of Sulamith, in which she criticized the lack of serious-ness among Jews towards their religion.

Henrietta's night school for Russian immigrants (as in the story) was one of the first schools for grown-ups in America. She held classes in a loft.

When Henrietta went to Palestine in 1920, she planned to stay only two years, but instead she stayed for twenty-four. She put her whole heart and soul into her work, beginning the day at 5:30 in the morning and stopping work at 11:30 at night.

Henrietta Szold died in 1945, having devoted her entire life to making other people healthy and happy.

15

"My People Shall Return"

JANUARY 5, 1895
Paris, France

To the Editor
New Free Press
Vienna, Austria

Here is my story on the trial of Captain Dreyfus, although what I saw today was so shocking and so terrible that I can scarcely describe it. Never in all my years as a newspaperman have I seen anything like it.

Paris was cold and grey today. Only army officers and their wives and a few of us newspapermen were allowed to enter the grounds of the Military Academy. Hundreds of people pressed against the iron gates, pushing and struggling to get a glimpse of what went on.

Five thousand soldiers lined up stiffly, forming a square in the middle of the field. It was bitter, freezing cold. The General sat on his horse in the center of the massed men. A little after nine o'clock, Captain Dreyfus was led out by four soldiers. They marched him across the great field and halted before the General. In a voice which cut through the cold grey air like a knife, the General said:

"Alfred Dreyfus, you are not worthy to bear arms. You are a traitor to France. In the name of France, I take away your rank as an officer!

"Let the sentence be carried out!"

Dreyfus lifted his right arm. His voice rang out: "I swear that you punish an innocent man! Long live France!"

The great, booming drums rolled. It was an angry, frightening sound. The officer in charge ripped the buttons and cords from Dreyfus' coat. He was no longer an officer in the French Army. He stood condemned as a traitor to his country.

Flanked by guards on either side, Dreyfus was marched around that huge square, past five thousand soldiers standing stiffly with their faces averted from him. As he passed the rows of soldiers he cried out again and again:

"I am innocent! Long live France! Long live the army!"

It was heartbreaking. Again and again he cried out, his voice growing hoarser and hoarser, and not a single human face was turned to him in pity. As he came closer to the newspaper men, he paused for an instant and looked at us.

"Tell all France I am innocent," he said, his voice breaking. I felt as though he spoke to me, alone.

When the mob outside the gates caught sight of Captain Dreyfus, a wave of hatred seemed to sweep over them.

"Death to the traitor!" they howled. "Bring him out here and we'll tear him to pieces! Death to the Jews! Death to the Jews!"

These people were like madmen. I believe they would have torn Dreyfus apart if the guards had not hurried him off to prison.

I hear he is to be sent to Devil's Island. He can hardly survive there, I am sure. The men lead terrible lives—the burning sun, the wretched food, the back-breaking labor.

The charges against Dreyfus are false. I do not believe he could ever have given French secrets to the Germans. No Jewish officer on the staff of the French army could do such a contemptible thing. How he loved his country and the army! He could never have betrayed France.

I don't think Dreyfus fully understands what has really happened. Of course, he knows that he has been disgraced and thrown into prison, that his trial was false, based on lies. But I do not think he realizes what is beneath all this.

Think—think of what actually happened. The crowd of good French citizens pounded against the gates and screamed "Death to the *Jews!*" They meant death to *all* Jews because one Jew is supposed to be a traitor. I could see the hatred on their faces as they cursed him, while the buttons and medals were being torn from his coat.

This did not happen in some simple little village in a backward country where one would expect ignorance and prejudice. It happened in Paris, in the "City of Light," the capital of the country which is supposed to stand for liberty, democracy, equality; the city of art and learning and love of freedom. And it happened a hundred years after the French Revolution and the French Declaration of the Rights of Man.

What I saw today has taught me a very important lesson, one which Jews everywhere should learn. I have not been much of a Jew before today. Like so many of my friends and colleagues, I've been too busy trying to be a success to pay much attention to being a Jew. The truth is, I suppose, I've really tried to run away from it—I even thought of becoming a Christian.

But if what I saw today can happen in France, the cradle of democracy, then no Jew is truly safe anywhere. It is not merely a question of Captain Dreyfus and the shame and humiliation which has been heaped upon his head. If even the French can feel this hatred for Jews, then I must find another way to make all Jews free, equal and as safe as other men. What I saw today has changed the whole course of my life.

I do not know how much of this you will print. Use what you like.

Theodor Herzl

JUNE 2, 1895
Paris, France

To the Editor
New Free Press
Vienna, Austria

I have thought a great deal about the Jewish problem

since I reported the Dreyfus case. The Jews are scattered all over the world. We are never sure of how we will be treated in the countries where we live because we have no homeland of our own. We need a place where we can control our own destiny, a place where Jews can help each other, where Jews who are not treated decently can find a home and enjoy the same rights as other men.

We have not had a homeland for over eighteen hundred years. The kind of plan I have in mind needs the loyal help of many men, and we shall need millions of dollars. Where is the money to come from? I began to think.

Now, Baron Maurice de Hirsch is here in Paris. He is an enormously rich man. He has bought large farms in Argentina where he helped Jews from Eastern Europe settle as farmers. But I have a plan which is very different from his. I was eager to discuss it with him. Thinking that he would surely understand and be willing to help, I asked to see him.

This afternoon I was shown into the paneled study of his luxurious home in Paris. The Baron, who wears a large, pointed mustache, looked up from behind his huge desk. Hopefully, I began.

"I know you are a good Jew, Baron, and a very generous man. But charity does not solve the basic problem of our people. What we need is a far-reaching plan for the future. All Jews must be educated more, to—"

The Baron was appalled at this.

"No, no!" he said, his mustache quivering. "Enough education! Much of our trouble comes from aiming too high, much too high!"

"But you don't understand," I hastened to explain. "I

propose that the Jews be educated to the idea of a homeland of our own, perhaps in Palestine. If we say to the rulers of the countries in which we live, and live unequally with the Christians—'Let us go! We do not belong here. Let us have our own homeland!' Jews will be respected everywhere."

The Baron shrugged. "Where will you get the money? Wealthy Jews won't give it to you for such a harebrained scheme."

"Then I shall create a national loan for ten million dollars."

"You are mad," he said. "Your plan is wild, fantastic. And besides, this idea smacks a little too much of politics to me. But wait," he said, putting his hand upon my arm as I rose to go, "this is not the end. We will talk of this again."

And that was how it went. Naturally, I was deeply disappointed. I talked it over with my friend Emil Schiff, who is a doctor. He, too, seemed to think me mad. He told me that my mind had begun to crack, that I needed rest. He even gave me a prescription and told me to take it for my nerves. He said that I was acting like a fool, that my idea was hopelessly impractical.

But I tell you that history will prove me right. I will organize the people. If the rich Jews will not give their dollars, the poor Jews will give their pennies—and there are certainly more poor Jews than rich ones. We will create a national fund. For the first time in hundreds of years, we will give Jews the chance to choose what they want to do with their lives. The people, the masses of the people, are our only hope.

We must begin now! Our people must be free to build

"You are mad," he said. "Your plan is wild, fantastic."

their own homeland. It may take years, but it took Moses forty years to bring the Israelites into the Promised Land. No matter how long it may take, I shall work for the day of Jewish freedom. And the day will come when Jews will once again enter the Promised Land.

Herzl

DECEMBER 1, 1895
Vienna, Austria

To the Editor
New Free Press
Vienna, Austria

I have assembled the thoughts which I have been writing you and put them into a little book called *The Jewish State*. After I had seen and spoken with many people, I realized that I must reach more of them, that I must put my ideas into a book. For five days I have been writing, barely stopping to eat or sleep.

I know now that I am not crazy. When I told my ideas to Dr. Max Nordau, the psychologist, he understood at once. He promised to do all he could to help me. In England I met Israel Zangwill, the famous writer. He liked my plan. So did Lieutenant Goldsmith, who had been raised as a Christian. He returned to our people after he was already a grown man. When he heard my plan, he cried, "This is my life's dream! We shall work for the liberation of Israel!"

I hope you will understand my excitement. At last I am making some progress with my plans for the future of our people!

Let me tell you some of the ideas in my little book, *The Jewish State*.

It would be stupid of us to deny that the Jewish problem exists. Many people in many countries do not like Jews and do not want them to have real freedom. The problem cannot be solved a little bit at a time or differently in different countries. It is a problem for all Jews.

We Jews are a people. Those who try to become more and more like Gentiles, who try to reduce Judaism to a few beliefs, are still known as Jews no matter where they live or how un-Jewish they may become.

No matter how much we contribute to the life of our adopted countries, there are always those who fear and hate us. Consider the fate of Captain Dreyfus. Two years have passed and he still rots in prison, perhaps more dead than alive.

If Jews could vanish as a people, completely, there would be no problem. But even if that were possible, it is not a proper solution. We *wish* to remain Jews. I say that the Jew who desires to lose himself, or to become a Gentile, may do so. But the Jewish people cannot, must not and will not cease to be.

We need an exodus, as in biblical times. I wish to organize the Jews of the world to help those who need or desire to go to the new Jewish homeland. I call this movement Zionism—the return to Zion.

I end the book:

Let the word be repeated here which was given at the beginning: the Jews who will it, shall have their state. We shall at last live as free men on our own soil, and die peacefully in our own homeland. The world will be made free by our freedom, made rich by our wealth, made greater by our greatness. And that which we seek there for our own use will stream out for all men.

Herzl

August 31, 1897
Basle, Switzerland

To the Editor
New Free Press
Vienna, Austria

The first Zionist Congress is not quite over but I must write of it. Though I am worn out from lack of sleep, I am so happy about what has happened that I must set it down at once.

It began three days ago when Dr. Lippe struck the table three times with his gavel. The two hundred and four delegates were elegant gentlemen all, splendidly dressed, each in frock coat and white tie. They had come from every corner of the globe. The great concert hall was crowded with members of the Congress from Russia, Germany, Austria-Hungary, from Bulgaria and Roumania, from England, Holland, Belgium, from Palestine, from Sweden and Denmark, from America, and from Algeria. The doors were hung with a flag with a white field, two blue stripes, and the Star of David. The galleries were filled with visitors, newspaper men, and many Christians, who understood and sympathized with the grand plan.

There has been nothing like this meeting in almost two

thousand years of Jewish history. Not since the great Sanhedrin met in Jerusalem has there been a congress to speak for all our people. We did not hide or meet in secret as the Zionists have had to do in some countries. We speak out, unafraid, as men fighting for their rights, and say to all who will listen, "The Jewish people want a Jewish state." We know this will not hurt us, but can only help us. It will give Jews everywhere pride, courage, strength—and it will bring many non-Jews to our side to help.

The vast crowd fell silent as Dr. Lippe said the prayer: "Blessed art Thou, O Lord our God, Ruler of the world, Who has kept us alive, sustained us, and brought us to witness this day."

When I rose and walked to the platform, there was silence. Then the people began to clap. They applauded for fifteen minutes, clapping, waving their handkerchiefs, cheering. They were clapping not for me, but for the idea, the hope for a new life for our people.

"We are here to lay the foundation stone of the house which is to shelter the Jewish nation," I told them. "Some people still hate us. But this has merely served to make us strong. We have returned home. Zionism means the return of the Jews to Judaism even before their return to the Jewish land."

During the three days here many things were discussed. Not everyone agreed on everything, but I am happy to say that the Congress did decide on a clear statement of the aims of the Zionist movement: "Zionism seeks to secure a publicly recognized, legally secured home in Palestine for the Jewish people."

166

At the closing of the Congress, Professor Max Mandelstamm, one of the oldest men present, reminded the delegates that they would have to work hard for many years to build the Jewish national home in Palestine. He warned of the danger and opposition and of a long, long struggle. But every man there was determined to succeed. Shouts and applause broke out once more. The dignified Englishman, Israel Zangwill, jumped up on one of the tables, clapping with all his might. The Congress closed in the midst of great joy.

If you asked me what I accomplished here I would have to say, "In Basle I founded the Jewish State." If I said this out loud everyone would laugh at me. But perhaps in five years, certainly in fifty, everyone will see it.

Can I do it? Can I bring this people to a new way of life? Can I lead them to be a proud, independent, free nation once more? Who would dare to do such a thing? But how can I *not* try? And with the people united behind me in the Zionist Congress, I cannot fail.

For as long as I shall live this will be my whole goal—to work for the future of Zionism!

Herzl

What Do You Think?

Baron de Hirsch meant to help his people; Theodor Herzl meant to help his people help themselves. What was the difference in their plans?

Something for You to Do

A collection of Theodor Herzl's letters is to be put into book form and you have been asked to design the cover of that book. Draw such a cover.

You Will Enjoy Reading

"The Story of a Dream That Came True." *Great Jews Since Bible Times*, by ELMA E. LEVINGER, Behrman House, Inc., p. 151.
"The Traitor" and "Without Messiah," *Giants on the Earth*, Part II, by DEBORAH PESSIN, Behrman House, Inc., pp. 45-61.
Theodor Herzl, by DEBORAH PESSIN, Behrman House, Inc.
"If I Forget Thee," *The Great March*, Book II, by ROSE G. LURIE, Union of American Hebrew Congregations, p. 202.

Some More Facts About Theodor Herzl

Theodor Herzl was born in Budapest in 1860, but moved to Vienna as a boy. Herzl studied law. Suddenly his interest changed. He became a reporter in Paris for the Viennese newspaper, *Neue Freie Presse*. At the same time he wrote plays for the Viennese theater.

When Herzl developed his idea of Zionism (the Jews to work for a Jewish national homeland), he made it part of politics, not just a religious hope. Herzl and his family had little interest in Judaism as a religion.

Herzl was received by the German Kaiser and the Sultan of Turkey. He even got the British Colonial Secretary, Joseph Chamberlain to agree to the settlement of Jews in British East Africa. But the Zionists wouldn't accept that in place of Palestine and the British lost interest in the idea. Herzl made the Zionist idea important to many countries and to most Jews.

Just before Herzl died in 1904, he wrote a prediction in his diary—that a Jewish state would be in existence in fifty years, and in 1948 it was.

168

RABBI STEPHEN S. WISE

The Free Pulpit

SIX men sat around a table in a meeting room of Temple Emanu-El in New York. At one end sat Rabbi Stephen S. Wise, straight and tall, his strong jaw set firmly. He listened with great seriousness as Louis Marshall, honorary secretary of the temple, opened the meeting.

"Rabbi Wise," Marshall smiled, "what would you expect of us if we decided to elect you rabbi of this temple?"

The young rabbi spoke clearly in a deep voice. "You invited me to speak here because you have heard of the new ideas I introduced to my congregation in Oregon. Whatever I have succeeded in doing there has been done because from the very beginning I told the congregation quite clearly

169

'This pulpit must be free.' The same must hold true here, for I could accept the call to be your rabbi only if I am free to speak on whatever problems I feel to be most important."

The smile faded from Louis Marshall's face. "Dr. Wise," he replied, "I must say at once that your condition is impossible. The pulpit of this temple always has been and will be under the control of the Board of Trustees."

"In that case, Mr. Marshall, I cannot be your rabbi. There is nothing more to say."

"Don't be in such a rush to decide," one of the other men broke in. "Just what do you mean by a free pulpit?"

Rabbi Wise turned to him. "Let me give you some examples. *If* a member of the temple ran for public office as the choice of a crooked political machine, I would publicly oppose his election. *If* some of you people own mines and children work in them, as Temple Emanu-El's rabbi I would protest in the pulpit against such child labor. *If* other members of the temple in the insurance business do not wish the state to examine their affairs, I would still urge the investigation of insurance crimes."

"But we are hiring a rabbi, not a prophet!" cried one member of the committee. "Our rabbi must represent *us*."

Rabbi Wise stood up. He looked very tall and lean as he towered above the others. "It is the rabbi's task to interpret God's word. Sometimes he must point out the difference between what men desire for themselves and what God demands from us. Thank you, gentlemen, and good day."

The members of the committee sat in amazed silence as Rabbi Wise closed the door behind him, having just refused to serve as rabbi for one of the most important temples in

170

the United States. Outside, his wife Louise took both his hands as she searched his face for his answer. "No need to tell me, Stephen," she smiled. "I can see in your eyes that you said no."

"I had to, Louise. There is no freedom for a rabbi here. As someone once said, 'Temple Emanu-El lives under *Marshall* law."

Louise laughed. "What a pun, Stephen!"

"But Louise, I told them the truth. I said that I could not become their rabbi under such conditions."

Louise pressed his hands in hers. "You had no choice. Let's go to the hotel and get ready for the trip back to Oregon."

"Right," the rabbi said as they left the temple. "But I shall come back to New York one day and start a new synagogue. And it will be entirely free in every way."

True to his word, Rabbi Wise soon resigned from the temple in Portland. He and Louise and their little children, Justine and James, returned and settled in New York. The family was soon very busy—Louise arranging their new home, the children getting used to the strange sounds and sights of the great city, and Rabbi Wise meeting with people who might help him form a new kind of congregation.

In 1907 the new temple was established. Rabbi Wise called it the "Free Synagogue."' At first its members met in the Hudson Theatre. Then they moved to the Universalist Church. Later they held services in Carnegie Hall which was a very large auditorium, but not too large to seat the hundreds of people who came to hear Rabbi Wise preach and to pray with his new congregation.

Over the years, Rabbi Wise built a synagogue which was truly free. He was free to say whatever he felt must be said, even if it wasn't always the popular thing. He led the fight for the rights of poor people. He staunchly supported the cause of honest city government.

The synagogue was free to rich and poor alike. There were no reserved seats. Each member gave what he could to support the work of the synagogue and all were welcome to come. People who did not have much money were treated the same way as those who were wealthy.

Rabbi Wise was rabbi of the Free Synagogue for over forty years.

In 1919, the members of the Free Synagogue decided to build their own temple. A building fund was begun and a great many people promised to give money.

During the same year several hundred thousand workers in steel factories went on strike. The workers wished to form a union so that they could bargain together for more pay, shorter hours of work, and better conditions in the factories. The factory owners fought this, sometimes hiring gangsters to beat up and terrify the labor leaders.

Rabbi Wise had to decide whether to speak publicly about the strike. He knew that if he did speak in favor of the strikers, many people would cancel their pledges to the temple building fund. Others might leave the congregation. At that time, the idea of labor unions was new to our country. Some people mistakenly thought the labor union leaders communists. Others believed that if workers earned more, the owners would not make enough money to stay in business. Members of the synagogue who employed workers did not wish them to unite in unions and grow stronger. But Rabbi Wise thought the steel workers had the right to join together to improve the conditions under which they worked. He felt that if he did not speak the truth as he saw it, he would fail in his duty as rabbi.

The Sunday morning after Yom Kippur, Rabbi Wise and Louise walked along Fifth Avenue to the temple service. The rabbi walked quickly, but Louise lingered at the shop windows filled with new fall clothes. "Why are you in such a hurry?" she asked. "We have plenty of time."

"I might as well get it over with," he answered. "Louise, my sermon this morning will light a million dollar fire."

Louise understood what he meant. "You have decided to speak on the steel strike?"

"Yes. When I'm through telling them how I feel about the workers, we'll be lucky if there is any congregation left!"

That morning Carnegie Hall was packed. After the first part of the service was over, Rabbi Wise strode determinedly to the center of the platform. He looked very tall in his Prince Albert coat and striped trousers. His voice was firm and deep as he spoke. He told his congregation about the miserable working conditions in the steel mills. He described what it meant for a man to work ten or twelve hours a day, such long hours that he seldom saw his own children when they were awake. He spoke about the private policemen hired by factory owners to break into the homes of union leaders and beat them up on the streets.

Rising to his full height, Stephen Wise stood quietly for a moment before the great crowd that jammed the hall. He

173

ran his hand through his thick black hair, then pointed directly at the crowd. In a voice like thunder he called out, "The World War we have just finished was won just as much by workers in the steel mills of Pennsylvania as by American soldiers in France. Now the heads of industry have set out to undo the workers' gains! The workers are not free to organize! They are not free to express themselves! I charge the United States Steel Corporation with the use of force and violence to break the strike!"

Louise looked nervously about her. Some people were so surprised at the rabbi's words that their mouths hung open. Others nodded their heads in agreement. But many scowled darkly and whispered to each other.

It was soon clear that Rabbi Wise was a prophet in more ways than one. Many people did cancel their promises of money for the building fund. Others resigned from the Free Synagogue.

In the midst of this storm of protest Rabbi Wise wrote to the officers of the Free Synagogue offering to leave. He felt that if a rabbi was free to speak his mind, the congregation was also free to choose another rabbi if they wished.

The officers refused his resignation. They held that the pulpit must remain free, that the rabbi speaks not just *for* but *to* the congregation. Thus, the fight ended happily—but as Rabbi Wise had feared, so many people refused the money they had promised that the hope of a new temple building was lost.

During and after the First World War, Woodrow Wilson was President of the United States. Rabbi Wise admired

174

President Wilson because he tried to do what was right and good for all Americans. Woodrow Wilson knew that workers had a right to form unions and to bargain together to improve their working conditions.

Meanwhile, the Zionist movement was growing among Jews throughout the world. More and more Jews had left unhappy homes in Europe to settle in Palestine with the help of Zionists in other countries.

In 1913, Rabbi Wise, one of the world leaders of Zionism, had visited Palestine. Palestine was then under Turkish rule. The Turks had compelled him to sign a document promising that he would remain in Palestine only a few weeks. By this means the Turks limited the number of Jews permitted to settle in Palestine.

Towards the end of the First World War, England promised to help the Jewish people establish a national home in Palestine. Rabbi Wise knew that a letter from President Wilson, declaring to all the world that he was in favor of a Jewish national home in Palestine, would be of great help to the Zionist cause, especially in the eyes of the English.

Rabbi Wise requested and was granted a meeting with the President at the White House. Woodrow Wilson, a tall thin man, looked tired and worn from the cares of his great office, but he smiled warmly as he shook the rabbi's hand.

"I have heard that you worked in a shipyard to help win the war. Now I know that it must be true, because you have the grip of a shipyard laborer."

The two men got quickly to what concerned them most: the problems which faced their country. Rabbi Wise reminded the President of the Balfour Declaration, England's promise of a homeland for the Jews. "Mr. President," he said, "you understand the miserable conditions under which Jews live in many parts of the world. We Zionists hope to help them settle in Palestine. We believe that, once we have a national home, the Jewish people will also make a contribution to the world. We shall build a nation to help others as well as ourselves.

"We need a word of support from you, the President of the United States. It would help greatly if you would give us a statement in support of the Balfour Declaration and the Zionist movement."

A few days later, just before the eve of Rosh Ha-shono, the Jewish New Year, Rabbi Wise received this letter

August 31, 1918

My dear Rabbi Wise:
I have watched with deep and sincere interest the work which has been done in Palestine at the instance of the British Government. I welcome an opportunity to express the satisfaction I have felt in the progress of the Zionist movement in the United States. I note that all America will be happy to learn that the foundation of the Hebrew University of Jerusalem has already been laid.
Cordially and sincerely,
Woodrow Wilson

All his life Rabbi Wise spoke and worked for the growth of Jewish life in Palestine which today is the State of Israel.

Rabbi Wise had many close friends and fellow workers among the rabbis trained at the Hebrew Union College in Cincinnati. He knew and admired the great work which this school had done for the Jews of America and the world. As the years passed, however, he came to feel that there should also be a school for liberal Jewish learning, and for training rabbis, in New York City. This was the largest Jewish community in the world, the center of Zionism, the home of America's leaders, the city where problems of the Jewish people and of the nation were discussed and historical decisions were made.

Although he was rabbi of the Free Synagogue, he attended countless political meetings, spoke and worked for many groups of people and was the leader of the Zionist Organization of America. Despite his great responsibilities, the school must be founded. He set to work on the new project, and in 1922 the Jewish Institute of Religion opened its doors in New York to future young rabbis.

For over twenty-five years Rabbi Wise served as President of the school. In 1949 his seminary and the school in Cincinnati joined and became known as the Hebrew Union College-Jewish Institute of Religion. Through his life and his work, he had shown what an American rabbi must be—one who loves his people, his freedom and, always, the truth.

What Do You Think?

A book company is planning to publish books on Theodor Herzl, Isaac Mayer Wise and Stephen S. Wise. They have decided on the following titles for two of the books:

Isaac Mayer Wise, The Builder of the Hebrew Union College and the Union of American Hebrew Congregations.
Theodor Herzl, The Founder of Modern Zionism.

What would you suggest as a title for the book on Stephen Wise?

Stephen Wise, The. . . .

Something for You to Do

Design a stamp that might be issued by the State of Israel and/or the United States in honor of Stephen S. Wise.

See the filmstrip *Rabbi Stephen S. Wise: A Twentieth Century Prophet.*

Some More Facts About Stephen S. Wise

Stephen Wise was born in Budapest in 1862 and was brought to the United States as an infant. He became a rabbi at the age of twenty-one, after assisting at New York City's Congregation B'nai Jeshurun only a year. In 1900 he was called to serve Beth Israel in Portland, Oregon.

Among the new ideas which Wise instituted when he founded the Free Synagogue (see the story) were: a social service division, a factory to give tubercular patients part-time work, and a child-adoption center. In 1913 almost half of the synagogue's dues was devoted to helping the needy.

Wise's free pulpit brought attacks upon injustice wherever it occurred. When New York City's mayor, Jimmy Walker, tried to raise his own salary, Wise angrily brought the matter out into the open. The mayor received not a penny more.

Wise fought, too, against racial discrimination and became one of the founders of the National Association for the Advancement of Colored People.

American Jewry lost a great man when Stephen S. Wise died in 1949.

17

RABBI LEO BAECK
Upright Before Men

On YOM KIPPUR eve of 1936, the Jews of Germany went to their synagogues with hearts full of sadness and fear. The country had fallen under the rule of the Nazi party, a gang of political hoodlums and murderers who had gained control of the country by violence and deceit. The Nazi leader, Adolf Hitler, one of the most evil men in history, had laid down a government policy which was meant to turn the attention of the German people away from their real political problems and to strengthen their faith in him; it put the blame for all Germany's poverty and misgovernment upon the Jewish people.

Jewish children had been driven from the public schools.

Jewish citizens were robbed of their property. Many of them were thrown into prison without any reason.

As the sun set, the Jews of Berlin, the capital of Germany, thronged the Liberal synagogues for the Kol Nidrei service. They gathered to pray to God for help and to hear what Rabbi Leo Baeck, the chief Liberal rabbi of Berlin, might have to say to them in this dark time of trouble and danger.

Rabbi Baeck was a very tall man, somewhat bent from years of study. He stood before his people, his silvery hair shining and his eyes alert and unafraid behind the thick glasses. He spoke so clearly that every word carried to the farthest corners of the temple.

"I speak as head of the German Rabbi's Association and of the National Association of German Jews. I have prepared a prayer which will be read tonight in every synagogue in Germany." He paused. "The congregation will please rise."

"In this hour every Jew stands before the Lord, the God of mercy and justice, to open his heart in prayer. . . . Let us admit our sins. But let us declare that the things said against us and our faith are lies. Let us trust God. We bow our heads before God and remain upright and erect before men."

A great sigh went through the congregation. Yes, they thought, his words are true.

But Frau Nathalie Baeck, the rabbi's wife, trembled with fear as her husband spoke his courageous words. She knew the Nazis would hear of his defiance. What would they do to him?

And as she feared, they came the day after Yom Kippur. The Nazi police took the rabbi to a Berlin prison for questioning.

"Dr. Baeck," the short, cruel-faced man addressed him insolently, "you are the leader of the Jews in Germany. Is that right?"

Rabbi Baeck looked at him with great dignity. "I have the honor of serving as head of our community, yes. But we Jews are not like you Nazis. Our real leader is God."

The short man began to flush with anger. "You wrote the prayer which was read in all the synagogues, in which you said that we Nazis lied about the Jews. Is that true?"

"Yes, it is true," said the rabbi calmly. "It is both true that I wrote the prayer and that you have lied about us."

The Nazi turned dark red and began to sputter with anger. "Guard!" he called. "Take this man away!"

The guard clicked his heels, saluted stiffly and said "Heil Hitler!" He seized Rabbi Baeck roughly by the arm and led him off to a prison cell. But the Nazis did not dare to imprison him for long; he was too well-known in other countries to risk the protest which this would cause.

Rapidly, the situation in Germany grew worse and worse for the Jewish people. And Rabbi Baeck, while he suffered their pain and humiliation, had his own unhappiness to bear. For the next year Frau Baeck became ill. She worried daily about her husband; she feared what the Nazis might do to him for his courage and defiance. Each day she grew weaker; not long after she died. Though old friends tried to comfort Rabbi Baeck, he was always to mourn her loss.

"She was my dearest friend and companion," he said. "Her death is for me the hardest of all these hard blows."

But the painful hard days had just begun for the Jews. In 1938, the Nazis set fire to all the synagogues in Germany.

They would not permit Jews to buy food. Thousands of them were rounded up like cattle and herded into huge prisons called concentration camps, specially built for policing thousands of people, young and old.

When the burning of the synagogues became known outside Germany, a congregation in the United States cabled Rabbi Baeck, inviting him to come to America at once. But he replied, "As long as there is a single poor Jew left alive in Germany, my place is with him." Then Rabbi Baeck called a meeting of the National Association of German Jews. "The end is near," he told them. "We must work hard and fast. Let us prepare the children and young people to leave Germany as soon as possible. Let us work to educate and keep up the courage of the older people. Many will have to stay and bear whatever comes. Our friends in England and America will help us save the children and get them out of Germany."

Others prepared to follow Rabbi Baeck's plan. They knew they could count on their rabbi and they were proud of his fearless courage.

The plans for moving the children went forward swiftly. Several groups of young people were sent to England, where Jews and Christians together worked to find homes for them. The parents were sick at heart as they kissed their boys and girls good-bye. Many children cried at leaving their mothers and fathers. The excitement of a train ride and a boat trip across the English Channel could not cheer them. No one knew what would happen to the Jews who remained in Germany.

One day the rabbi's friend, Hans Cohen, said gravely, "Rabbi, it looks like war, another world war. You know what that will mean for us. It won't be like the last war when you served our people as a chaplain for four years in the German army. That is all forgotten. Once war begins, the Nazis will no longer need to hide their crimes against us from the world. It will mean the end for those of us still left in Germany."

"Yes," the rabbi said, "I know it is coming. England, America, and other countries have been weak and slow to act against Germany. But the Nazis have finally gone too far— there will be war."

"Then we must speed our plans to help as many Jews as possible to leave Germany. We must save the children. Another group is about to depart for England." Cohen spoke carefully. "We need . . . a leader for this group. The children are afraid of the journey. Something could go wrong on the way. Leo, I know how busy you are. But I . . . that is, we . . . we thought *you* should go with the children this time. I have the tickets here." He took a thick envelope filled with railway and steamship tickets from his pocket and gave it to the rabbi.

Rabbi Baeck smiled kindly. "I think I know what you would like me to do, Hans. I'll go with the children."

Hans Cohen gave a sigh of relief. "At least our rabbi will be safe," he thought.

Hurriedly, Rabbi Baeck made ready for the trip to England. The next day he went to the railway station. Fifty children waited for him, some with their parents. "Don't come through the gates," the rabbi told the parents. "It will make the parting harder. Say good-bye here and try not to cry."

The parents tried to do as he said. Several even managed to smile when one little boy pulled at the rabbi's coat and called out, "I know you! You're Rabbi Baeck! I'm going to England with you for a visit!"

"Yes, my boy, you are. And do you know what I have in this suitcase? Candies—for everyone who behaves well." The rabbi spoke to the children "Come now, quickly! We must not miss the train!"

The rabbi led the children through the gates to the tracks. The train waited; several passenger cars with a long, black bullet-shaped engine. The children climbed into the two last cars. A whistle blew and the train moved out of the station, headed for Le Havre in France. From there the rabbi and his little group took a boat across the English Channel and another train to London. In London, they were met by people from the Central British Fund Agency. The children said good-bye to Rabbi Baeck and were led to buses. One of the British men stayed behind to talk to Rabbi Baeck.

"Will you come to a meeting, Rabbi?" he asked. "It will help if we can discuss plans for the children with you."

Rabbi Baeck smiled his kind, wise smile. "Of course, I will come," he said.

After the plans had been discussed, the chairman turned to Rabbi Baeck. "We are worried about you, just as your friends in Berlin are. Please stay in England with us. Everything is arranged. We fear for your safety."

"I thought you might suggest that," Rabbi Baeck nodded. "I knew what Hans Cohen had in mind when he asked me to bring the children here. Thank you, my friends, but I cannot remain. I must go back."

"Do you realize what great danger awaits you in Germany?" one man asked.

"Yes, I know. But I cannot leave my people at such a time."

"Is there anything we can do for you, Rabbi?"

"Yes, there is one thing. There is something I'd like to look up in the library of the British Museum. Please take me there and leave me alone for an hour or two."

The men looked at one another in astonishment. They could hardly believe their ears. Here was a man who had escaped from the terror of the Nazis and all he wanted was a chance to read something in the British Museum!

"Very well, Rabbi—if that is all you wish. But if you change your mind, and we beg you to, please let us know at once."

In the library, for two hours, Rabbi Baeck read quietly about events that had happened several thousand years ago. He took careful notes, put the papers in his briefcase and returned to the railway station. He took the train to the coast, and the boat to Le Havre. Then he boarded the train back to Berlin.

Rabbi Baeck returned to his people in their time of sorrow and danger.

After the Second World War began, things grew steadily worse in Germany. All Jews had to wear a yellow, six-pointed star on their clothing. Those Jews who were able to, fled from the country.

In 1942, the Nazis closed the famous Jewish school in Berlin where Rabbi Baeck still taught. By that time, there were only three students left in the school. The rest had either fled or been sent to concentration camps.

Many thousands of Jews were sent to these camps. Some were slave workers in mines and factories. As a result of long hours and poor food, they died, one by one. Those who were not strong enough to work were killed in large numbers.

Not all who suffered this way were Jews. Christians who dared to speak against Hitler and his Nazi gangs were also punished by slave labor or sudden death.

Most of the Germans ignored the terrible things that were happening to the Jewish people. But some few tried to show that they cared. Sometimes people secretly gave food to Rabbi Baeck. A German woman left a basket of fruit and vegetables at his door each week. One day in the crowded bus, a man stepped close to him and asked, "What is the next station?" Then he whispered, "I am from the country. I have put a few eggs in your pocket." Little things like this gave Rabbi Baeck and his people hope. They knew they were not completely deserted and forgotten, even in Germany.

On January 28, 1943, at a quarter to six in the morning, two strange men in plain clothes came to Rabbi Baeck's home. "We are the secret police," they said. "We have come to take you to the concentration camp."

The rabbi was not surprised. He explained calmly that he wished to write a letter to his daughter, Ruth, and to pay some bills. If they would wait an hour while he did these things, he told them, he would go quietly. Otherwise, they would have to carry him through the streets. They waited.

In the camp, Rabbi Baeck found conditions even worse

than he had expected. People were crowded in bunks four or five deep on a wall. Meals were of coffee made from acorns, watery soup, and stale bread. The camp was surrounded by barbed wire and a high wall bristling with soldiers and guns.

To humiliate the great Jewish leader, the Nazis made the sixty-nine-year-old rabbi do the work of a horse. They harnessed him to a garbage wagon and forced him to pull it through the mud. Every day, from early morning to late afternoon, the old rabbi had to work at this job. When he was asked later how he could stand such terrible work, he said, "You see, the other 'horse' was a famous writer and a wonderful person and we had many interesting discussions."

But even in the concentration camp Rabbi Baeck found ways to help his people. He collected slices of bread from those who were still fairly strong and gave them to the weak and sick. He started secret "classes for education" in the camp. Over eight hundred men came to hear one of his talks. He prayed with the sick and he comforted those who mourned the death of loved ones. He was a great example to his people of how a man can endure the most terrible treatment and still remain strong and kind and brave.

Rabbi Baeck often wondered why he was not put to death as so many others had been. And one day, passing by the camp office, he found out why. There he accidently was seen by Adolf Eichmann, one of the worst of the Nazis. Eichmann looked at the rabbi and said, "I thought you were dead!" Then Rabbi Baeck understood what had happened. Another rabbi whose name was spelled "Beck" had died in the camp. The Nazis had made a mistake! They had not known that *this* Leo Baeck was still alive!

Now that the mistake was discovered, Rabbi Baeck expected to be killed. But three years had passed since he had been imprisoned in the camp and the war was almost over. American, British, and French troops had landed on the continent of Europe and were driving east towards Germany. Russian troops were advancing towards the west. Germany was about to collapse.

On May 12, 1945, the Russians entered the concentration camp and freed the prisoners. Rabbi Baeck was put in charge of giving out food and medicine. The Russians offered to turn the German guards over to the Jews so that the Jews could punish their tormentors themselves. Rabbi Baeck refused. "We do not wish to become like them," he said. "Let there be fair trials."

A month later an American jeep drove into the camp. An army sergeant announced that he had come to take Rabbi Baeck to London. The rabbi thanked him kindly but explained that there were still many sick people in the camp who needed him. "Come back in a month," he said, "and I shall be ready to go with you."

A month later the sergeant returned and took Rabbi Baeck to the city of Prague. From there Leo Baeck took a plane to London where, once again, he could live as a free man.

Although he was now seventy-five years old and had spent three years at slave labor in the concentration camp, Rabbi Baeck continued to serve his people. He was elected president of the World Union for Progressive Judaism. Half of each year he lived in London, where he worked for the World Union. The other half he spent in the United States. He spoke to men and women everywhere, and everywhere he was loved and respected.

He was asked to teach at the Hebrew Union College in Cincinnati. He loved this work. The students knew how much he had done for the Jewish people. His great spirit deeply touched all who came to his classroom and his presence in the students' dormitory seemed to make it a holy place.

On the birthday of Abraham Lincoln, the Congress of the United States asked Rabbi Baeck to open the session with a prayer. Standing before the members of Congress, he bowed his head. This is part of what he said

> Our Father, our God, we pray unto Thee on this birthday of Abraham Lincoln, Thy servant. For the sake of this land he became a witness of humanity, a herald of Thy command and Thy promise. Reverently, I pray Thee to bless Congress, its men and its days. From the bottom of my heart I pray: God Bless America.

What Do You Think?

Suppose you were one of the first American soldiers to arrive at the concentration camp where Rabbi Baeck was and spoke to him. What might he have said to you?

Something for You to Do

Make a poster asking students in your school to contribute money for the Leo Baeck School in Israel. (Write to the National Association of Temple Educators, 838 Fifth Avenue, New York City, for information.)

See the filmstrip Dr. Leo Baeck: Man of Faith.

Some More Facts About Leo Baeck

Leo Baeck was born in Poland in 1873, the son of a rabbi. After studying in Breslau and Berlin, Baeck served as rabbi in the

German cities of Opeln and Dusseldorf, and from 1912 on, in Berlin.

Leo Baeck rapidly became a well known figure in German Jewish circles. In 1922 he was elected chairman of the German Rabbinical Association. He later held the office of Grand President of the B'nai B'rith.

A great scholar, Baeck felt that the moral teachings of Judaism did not change as time passed, but that its ceremonies could be changed to fit the times. He taught, too, that Judaism was mainly a religion of action and not one of feeling alone.

During Rabbi Baeck's stay in Theresienstadt concentration camp (see the story), his life was spared when the Nazi called out Rabbi *Beck* by error, and another rabbi answered to the name.

Leo Baeck died in 1956, after becoming Reform Judaism's spiritual leader throughout its worldwide movement.

18

CHAIM WEIZMANN

"For Myself, Nothing . . ."

FOUR men and a woman entered a fashionable restaurant in the Strand in London and sat down at a table. Charles Scott, editor of the newspaper, the *Manchester Guardian*, turned to Chaim Weizmann and said, "This is a special occasion. I have known you since the early days, in Manchester, Chaim. Let me order some wine. We should drink a toast to you."

The other two men, David Lloyd George and Arthur James Balfour, agreed. "Yes, in honor of Chaim!" Dr. Weizmann's wife, Vera, looked at him with love and pride. Dr. Chaim Weizmann, the great chemist, was a middle-aged man, partly bald. He had a small moustache and goatee, and deep-set eyes that seemed to see directly to the heart of every-thing. Now he was smiling, happy to be the honored guest at the little luncheon.

"You should not make so much of my work," Chaim Weizmann said. "It was a rather small thing which I discovered, but I'm glad it has proved useful in the war."

The wine was served. David Lloyd George lifted his glass and said to Weizmann, "Have it your way. But the allied struggle against Germany has been greatly helped by your new chemicals for making explosives. What can our government give you to show our appreciation for your work?"

Putting his glass down, Weizmann looked earnestly at Lloyd George. "For myself, nothing," he replied, "but something for my people." And he thought, "During the centuries it has happened, not too often, but still, it has happened that some man *suddenly*, in a position of importance, has been able to say, 'For myself, nothing, but for my people, yes. I have a request.'" Chaim heard those very words from his mouth as though they were an echo from long, long ago.

"Very good, Chaim," said Balfour, "let's drink to your fondest wish for your people!" They all sipped the red wine. "Chaim," Lloyd George spoke thoughtfully, "you have many friends in England. Since I am in charge of guns and am-munition for our armies, I know how important your work is. But that is not the main reason why we feel close to you.

"Charles Scott tells me that you have been a Zionist ever since you were a boy in Russia. We know how badly the Jews are treated there. We understand why it is necessary for the Jews to have a home in Palestine."

Chaim Weizmann's eyes shone with the age-old dream.

192

"For myself, nothing, but something for my people."

"For two thousand years our people dreamed of returning to Zion, our ancient home, the land of the Bible. Zionism is a world movement for the Jewish people, for Jews scattered throughout all nations."

Lloyd George replied, "You have said that the hope of the Jewish people depends on England's winning the war. You are right. But even if that were not the case, your loyalty to the cause of democracy has won you many friends in England."

As lunch was served, Chaim Weizmann described the Jewish hopes for the future. "The Turks who own Palestine now are allies of Germany. If we win the war, the Turks will be driven out of Palestine. There are already some Jewish colonies there—farms and towns built by people who escaped from eastern Europe. They have a very hard time of it. The land is poor. The trees are gone, the good earth washed away. The soil is stony. But the settlers have endured the hardship and are building up the land. We believe that the Jewish people can build a homeland there after the war."

James Balfour was thoughtful as he put down his knife and fork. "You have many friends here, Chaim. But let's admit that not everyone feels as you do about Zionism. Some of your own people right here in England oppose it."

"I know who you mean, James," Chaim smiled bitterly. "They are afraid. They don't work for the future of the Jews because they are more concerned for themselves than for their suffering brothers. But we cannot worry about them. There is too much to be done."

After lunch, David Lloyd George and James Balfour returned to their offices. Weizmann had given them a new understanding of the Jewish problem and a possible solution to it.

Chaim Weizmann had been a Zionist since his childhood days in a village near the town of Pinsk. He had attended all the Zionist Congresses except the very first. He had known Theodor Herzl. Weizmann knew that love of Zion was as old as the Jewish people. He also knew how Jews were attacked and insulted in eastern Europe. As a child, Weizmann had seen boys carried away from their parents to serve for twenty-five years in the army of the Russian Czar.

Herzl tried to win Palestine for the Jews by seeking the help of the Sultan of Turkey and other powerful men. But Weizmann believed that the Jewish people would have to help themselves. He was a practical Zionist. He believed that his people would win Palestine by settling as many Jews as possible there to build cities and villages. He also thought that Zionists throughout the world should teach everyone what Zionism meant. He worked and traveled unceasingly to raise money to carry out these ideas.

During 1917, Chaim Weizmann continued to experiment in his laboratory in London. By this time his friends had become the most influential people in England. David Lloyd George had risen to the powerful position of Prime Minister, and Lord James Balfour was Foreign Minister of England. The war, now in its third year, was not going well for England and her allies. The United States had entered the war on the side of England and France, but there were still very few American soldiers trained and ready for combat in battle.

It was necessary to keep the Suez Canal open for British

ships to get to the east. The British Prime Minister knew that England needed friends in Palestine to protect the Canal. England also wanted more support from America. It seemed to Lord Balfour and Lloyd George that a public statement on Jewish rights in Palestine might win friends and support for England. It would surely help the Jews, especially those in eastern Europe, about whom Chaim Weizmann had spoken.

The French and Italian allies approved this public statement. President Woodrow Wilson in the United States stated that he was strongly in favor of the plan. His friend, Rabbi Stephen S. Wise, had often spoken to him about the need of the Jewish people for a homeland and their historic rights to Palestine.

In April of 1917, Lord Robert Cecil, assistant to Lord Balfour, discussed this with Chaim Weizmann. "If there were a Jewish home there, Dr. Weizmann," he asked, "do you think the Jews would wish the British to help protect Palestine?"

Chaim Weizmann became very excited. He began pacing up and down in Lord Robert Cecil's office. "But that is just what we are waiting for!" he said. "Of course the British should protect Palestine! It will be a long time before the Jews can do that alone. If a statement is made in support of a Jewish homeland, Jews everywhere will fight even harder for an Allied victory. And your government will go down in history for having helped right an old wrong against the Jewish people."

On September 19, Prime Minister Lloyd George discussed the wording of such a statement with the British Cabinet.

The only Jewish member of the Cabinet arose to speak. "Gentlemen, I urge you not to make such a statement. Many Jews are not in favor of Zionism. I am an Englishman. If there is a Jewish homeland, some people may think that I belong in Palestine. What will happen to me then? Please do not make a statement about the Jews in Palestine!"

Lloyd George and James Balfour exchanged a glance. "I regret that you are so worried," they told the Jewish Cabinet member, "but we can quickly get another opinion. Dr. Chaim Weizmann is waiting in another room to learn of our decision. I shall send messengers to bring him here."

The messengers were sent. The members of the Cabinet waited. The messengers searched and searched. Ten minutes passed, then twenty, then a half hour. The messengers never did find Chaim Weizmann because he had gone out for a breath of the fine spring air. At last, the Cabinet had to go back to work. They could wait no longer. The statement about Palestine was dropped.

But it came up again. This time the wording was agreed upon, but the statement was not as strong as it might have been if only the messengers had found Chaim Weizmann that first time it was discussed. On November 2, 1917, the Balfour Declaration was announced by the British government. It said, in part: "His Majesty's Government views with favor the establishment in Palestine of a national home for the Jewish people. . . ." It also stated that the English would help build this home. It promised that nothing would be done to harm the people already living in Palestine or to change the way of life of Jews who lived in other countries throughout the world.

197

The Balfour Declaration was a great victory for the Zionist idea. It put one of the great nations of the world firmly behind the building of a Jewish home in Palestine. Because he had done so much to bring about the Balfour Declaration, Chaim Weizmann was shorty thereafter chosen head of the World Zionist Organization.

As the years passed, many Jews migrated to Palestine. Some went there because they wanted to be pioneers, to help with the hard work. Others went because they had no homes where they could live on equal terms with their neighbors. The Zionist movement grew. The Jewish National Fund raised money throughout the world, wherever Jews lived. They used this money to buy land in Palestine on which new immigrants could settle as farmers.

The Jews built roads. They dug deep wells to bring water to the thirsty ground. They drained marshes and planted trees. Gradually, the country was dotted with farms, towns and cities. Jewish doctors and nurses helped both Jews and Arabs. Jewish workers built houses and factories. They put in telegraph poles and strung wires from one end of the land to the other. Jewish teachers taught the children to read and speak Hebrew. They started schools and a Hebrew University. The land of Israel grew.

During World War II, many of the Jews who could escape from Germany went to Palestine. Chaim Weizmann was happy that there was a place for these homeless people to go. Millions of Jews died, but many thousands were saved because there was a refuge for them in Palestine.

During these many years, Chaim Weizmann worked steadily for Zionism. Even when he was older he could not retire, because the emergencies grew always greater. His wife, Vera, was constantly at his side, helping.

During the terrible war, young Jews from Palestine tried to save the Jews who were still in Europe. Some were dropped by parachute from planes behind enemy lines. A girl named Hannah Senesch made contact with Jews in the secret forces in Europe. Many people were taken out to Palestine by this brave girl and other young men and women in the Jewish underground.

Meanwhile, many of the Arabs in Palestine and some in the Arab lands nearby sided with the Germans in the war. They did all they could to drive the Jews out of Palestine. The Arabs attacked Jewish farms and villages, killed settlers, and destroyed forests.

At the end of the war, the British Government decided that in order to pacify the Arabs, Palestine should be divided into two parts, one for the Jews and one for the Arabs. By a vote of thirty-three to fourteen, the United Nations decided to divide Palestine and to give the smaller part to the Jewish people for their own state.

Chaim Weizmann, now an old man, was on one of his many trips to the United States when the thrilling news came. Immediately, he urged President Harry S. Truman to give American recognition to the new state which was about to be born. On May 14, 1948, the Jews in Palestine declared that a new state existed, the State of Israel. They took charge of the area and prepared to defend it against the Arabs. Just ten minutes after he had received the news of Israel's Declaration of Independence, President Harry Truman announced that the United States recognized the State of Israel.

Chaim Weizmann was still in New York, staying at the Waldorf-Astoria Hotel. Two days later he received a cable telling him that he had been elected the first president of the State of Israel. It seemed almost impossible to believe! The State of Israel existed and he, Chaim Weizmann, at seventy-four, after a lifetime of hope and work, was its first president! In honor of their distinguished guest, the Waldorf raised the flag of Israel, the blue and white flag with its six-pointed star, over the entrance of the hotel. Thousands of people saw it and cheered wildly.

The very next day, Chaim Weizmann flew to Washington to thank President Truman. "You will never know what this means to my people," the President of Israel said to the President of the United States. "We have waited and dreamed and worked for this event for two thousand years. By recognizing the State of Israel at once, you have helped us take our place among the nations of the world. Your act will never be forgotten."

President Truman smiled broadly. "Lots of people here were against it," he admitted, "including the striped-pants boys in our State Department and the big shots in the oil business. But I read the whole record, and I knew that you were right and they were wrong."

The two presidents shook hands. And President Chaim Weizmann left for Israel to take office in the new state and guide it through its perilous historical beginnings.

What Do You Think?

What other Jewish heroes have you met who had favors

coming to them personally and who chose favors to help their people instead of themselves? In what way can their deeds be compared to your giving money to Keren Ami *out of your own allowance?*

Something for You to Do

Write the headlines for the newspapers of your community announcing that Israel has been declared a state and Chaim Weizmann is its first president.

Go and visit the office of your community newspaper and ask to see the 1948 edition and compare it to your headline.

Show the filmstrip *The Story of Chaim Weizmann,* Jewish Education Committee of New York.

Some More Facts About Chaim Weizmann

Chaim Weizmann, the first president of the State of Israel, was born in Poland in 1874, one of eleven children. His father, Oizer, was a poor merchant.

Chaim studied chemistry, moving to England after finishing his studies. He taught at the University of Manchester from 1904 to 1916. With the coming of World War I, he entered the service of the British Navy as Director of Chemical Laboratories. Weizmann soon became world-famous for his work.

Shortly after the Balfour Declaration was made public (see the story), Chaim Weizmann became a powerful force in the Zionist movement.

But he disagreed with Herzl's idea of Zionism (see the story on Theodor Herzl). Weizmann wanted British protection over Palestine first, while settlements grew, then independence. Weizmann would accept only Palestine as the place for a Jewish national homeland.

When Chaim Weizmann died in 1952, he was buried at Rehovot, Israel, one of his favorite cities.

19

CHAIM NACHMAN BIALIK
Poet of the Jewish People

M Y FRIEND Shemarya insists that I write some notes about my life. I sometimes think that people who write about themselves are very conceited. Shemarya, my partner in the book publishing business, is also a writer. We are neighbors here in Tel Aviv, this bustling new city in Eretz Yisrael. But Shemarya is not a poet. Maybe that's why he thinks it is easy for me to write about myself. As a poet, I would much rather write about the wonderful world and the interesting people around us in this Jewish city. But Shemarya keeps after me every day. "Have you written anything about yourself, Chaim?" he asks. "You are the greatest Hebrew poet since Yehudah Ha-Levi. People want to know about your life." I am sure that Shemarya greatly exaggerates the importance of my poetry. But if I do make some notes, perhaps my friend will stop asking me about it every day.

The facts about my life. . . . one thing I remember clearly from the time when I was a boy. My grandfather—of blessed memory—sent me to the best school in Zhitomir, a district capital in the Ukraine. I soon was graduated from the study of Bible to the Talmud. But I was also interested in books in the Russian language, books about history and science. After I had finished reading the lesson in Talmud, I would hide one of the other books in the cover of the big Talmud. One night my grandfather came to my room.

"What are you studying so late at night, Chaim?" my grandfather asked. Before I could answer he looked over my shoulder and saw the hidden book. "Aha, a book in the Russian language! You know that good Jews aren't supposed to read such books."

"I know Grandfather, but let me explain," I said quickly. "I enjoy studies in Talmud, especially the stories about the rabbis. But I am also interested in many other things. I think I have learned about all I can here. I would like to go to a real Yeshivah, like the one in Berlin in Germany."

My grandfather stroked his beard thoughtfully. "I would never send you to Berlin. Jews there want to be just like everyone else. They forget that they are Jews and think of themselves as Germans. Still, you may be right about going to a better school. I'll think about it. Now, Chaim, at least promise me that you won't read these new books until after you have finished your Talmud lessons. And be sure to get enough sleep."

I promised, blew out the candle, said the *Shema*, and was soon asleep. But his discovery of the hidden book resulted in something wonderful for me. My grandfather *did* help me go away to school; not to Berlin, but to the Yeshivah at Volozhin.

I'll never forget how I felt when I arrived at the Yeshivah. There I was, just a red-headed boy from the country, in a *real* city school! I was dressed like the other *chasidim* in Zhitomir. I wore a long black coat, blue stockings, and sandals. My earlocks had never been trimmed, and were much longer than those of the other students at the Yeshivah. My classmates laughed at me at first. But I soon made friends, shortened my coat, and trimmed the earlocks to a more sensible length.

I learned a lot more about the Talmud at Volozhin. I also learned about other things. Here, too, I hid the modern books about science and history and read them secretly. But I noticed that many of the other boys did the same thing. I also remember spending a lot of time just walking in the woods and fields outside the city. In the fall of the year the leaves of the trees turned from green to red and yellow, rust and brown. Birds swarmed overhead, flying south. Peasants worked in the fields preparing for the coming of winter. I wandered around, dreaming about what I imagined life would be like in far-off Zion. I began to write poems about what I saw and thought.

After a year and a half at the Yeshivah, I decided to run away. I wanted to go to Odessa, that great city on the shore of the Black Sea. It was the center of modern Hebrew writing. I dreamed of meeting great writers like Ahad Ha-Am. I wanted to go on studying but, more than anything else, I wanted to write down my feelings about life, in poetry.

By the time I was ready to leave, it was no secret to anyone. A hundred students from the Yeshivah marched along the road with me until we came to the place where the stagecoach stopped. There we all waited, singing Hebrew songs, until the stagecoach creaked to a stop in a cloud of dust in front of the town tavern. A man called out: "Stage for Odessa!," threw my small bundle on top of the coach and said to me: "Climb in, little Jew, we can't wait here all day!" The driver cracked his whip. The horses broke into a trot, and I was on my way to Odessa!

Once in the great city, I was really lost. I loved the sounds and sights of the streets, but I had great trouble finding my way around. I was also very poor. I had to find some kind of work. One of my friends in Volozhin had come from Odessa. His father was a rabbi in the city. And it was a very good thing that I looked him up. The rabbi took me in, fed me, and gave me a letter of introduction to the Hebrew writer, Ahad Ha-Am. "Remember, Chaim," the rabbi told me, "Ahad Ha-Am is a very great writer. My son has written me about your poems. I think you should copy one out very neatly. Give it to Ahad Ha-Am to read. If he thinks it is good, he will surely help you."

I did just as the rabbi had said. I dressed carefully and put a neat copy of my poem, "Welcome to the Bird," in my pocket. I set out for the home of Ahad Ha-Am. The great writer opened the door himself. He was a slim man with a trim little goatee and glasses. He greeted me in Hebrew. "Shalom. Welcome, my boy. The rabbi has told me that

205

you are a friend of his son. So, you have left Volozhin to come to the city of Odessa. Come in. Sit down and we shall have a cup of tea. What is that paper you have in your hand?"

I was afraid and very shy, but it was too late to turn and run away. "It is a Hebrew poem about a bird. Could I read part of it to you, sir?"

"By all means," replied Ahad Ha-Am, "let me hear it."

Clearing my throat nervously, I read

> Do you bring me friendly greetings
> From my brothers there in Zion
> Brothers far yet near?
> O the happy! O the blessed!
> Do they guess what heavy sorrows
> I must suffer here?

"But that is very good," Ahad Ha-Am interrupted. "You write in a Hebrew style which is fresh and unusual. I want to see more of your work."

I remember the joy I felt because the great Hebrew writer liked my poem. He not only liked it, but he had it published in a magazine! He also found me a job teaching some young children. This meant that I could stay in Odessa and study. It all seems so long ago, but there is still a link with the past today. After many adventures, and after many years passed, Ahad Ha-Am also moved to Tel Aviv. Now he is a neighbor of Shemarya Levin's and of mine.

I never had much of a head for business, as my partner, Shemarya, will be more than willing to tell you. But ever since my first work in Odessa, I have managed to make a living at one job or another. Ahad Ha-Am invited me to some parties where I could meet other writers. One evening I met a lovely girl. Her name was Mania Averbach. Mania and I found that we had a great deal in common. We both loved the out-of-doors. And we both enjoyed reading, especially the new books by modern Hebrew authors. We fell in love and were soon married. I could not give Mania an expensive gift, so I wrote her a poem. Here is part of it, a poem about our marriage:

> Friend and kinsman, young and old,
> Shall be gathered to behold,
>> And with music and with mirth
>> They shall come to lead us forth.

> And the bridal canopy
> In this place shall lifted be.
>> I shall slip a ring of gold
>> On this finger that I hold,

> And pronounce the blessing: 'Thee
> God makes consecrate to me.'
>> And my enemies shall there
>> Burst with envy and despair.

Things went along pretty well for us until the Bolshevik Revolution broke out at the end of the World War. The poor people in Russia had suffered a great deal under their rulers, the Czars. A change was badly needed in Russia, but the new leaders of the revolution did evil things as well as good ones. They were against religion, our religion as well as all others. They had no understanding of the value of the Hebrew language. Knowing that Hebrew is the Jewish language of prayer, they opposed the teaching of Hebrew. They closed all of the Hebrew schools in Russia.

At that time I was preparing to publish the writing of a great Hebrew thinker and poet of the Middle Ages. His name was Ibn Gabirol. In my shop we had prepared the metal plates for the printing of that work. The leader of the new Secret Police in Odessa was a Jew named Deutsch. One day, while I was at work, a man banged on the door of the shop. "Open up! Open up in the name of the police," he called out. I opened the door and there stood Deutsch with four policemen.

"Hello, Deutsch," I said, "to what do I owe the honor of this visit?"

Deutsch did not return my greeting. Instead, he demanded rudely, in a loud voice: "Do you print Hebrew books here?"

"Yes, I do," I replied. "As you can see, all of these plates are for the texts of Hebrew books, including a new edition of the work of Ibn Gabirol, of whom you may have heard."

"Never mind about that Hebrew nonsense," Deutsch said. "You know that our revolutionary government has closed all Hebrew schools. We are against your religion and your language. But," he went on with a sly smile, "these plates here are made of excellent metal. We can use that metal to help build the new Russia." Turning to the policemen, he ordered: "Two of you go and get a truck. You other two come over here and start moving these plates outside. They will make good scrap metal."

What could I do? It broke my heart to see the precious plates being tossed into a pile in the street. I was out of business in Odessa.

The work of many years had been destroyed. There was no future for Jewish life or Hebrew writing in Russia. Mania

208

and I made up our minds to leave for Palestine. Ahad Ha-Am had already left to settle there in the new city of Tel Aviv. "Tel Aviv," I whispered to Mania, "that means Hill of Spring. It will be beautiful there. We shall begin all over again. Since Hebrew is the spoken language of the people there, I shall be able to work as editor and publisher in the language I love. There will be people able and anxious to read my poems." We made our plans very quietly because the Bolsheviks did not allow people to leave the country.

It was fortunate for me that I had been friendly with some of the best known Russian writers. One of the most famous, Maxim Gorki, went to the leader of the Communist Party to speak for me. He begged him to give me and Mania permission to move to Palestine. At last we were granted a permit. In great haste and joy Mania and I took a train to Berlin. From there we traveled to Palestine, where we have lived ever since. Here in Tel Aviv it is natural to live and write as a Jew. Here we have friends like Shemarya Levin and Ahad Ha-Am. And this is the only place in the world where Mania and I can sit on our balcony in the early evening and hear the children call to one another in Hebrew as they play their games.

Soon after we had settled here I received a great honor. Dr. Judah Magnes, President of the Hebrew University, asked me to give the main speech at the opening of the University. It was outdoors, in a natural theatre looking out over the wilderness of Judea, the Jordan Valley, with the blue mountains of Moab in the distance. The students had built a platform and some benches. Chaim Weizmann was one of the famous men who took part in the ceremony. Dr. Magnes had expected a small crowd. We were amazed when we saw over seven thousand people. They had come from all around the world. They sat on the ground in a vast semi-circle behind the few rows of benches. These are a few words from my speech on that great occasion:

> I am sure that the eyes of tens of thousands of Israel that are lifted from all parts of the world to this hill are shining with hope and comfort; their hearts and their flesh are singing a blessing of thanksgiving to the Living God Who hath preserved us and sustained us and let us live to see this hour. . . . We must therefore hasten to light here the first lamp of learning and science and of every sort of intellectual activity in Israel, ere the last lamp grows dark for us in foreign lands. And this we propose to do in the house whose doors have been opened this day upon Mount Scopus.

Well, this doesn't tell the complete story of my life, so far. But I do hope it will satisfy Shemarya so that we can get back to work. And there is much work to be done. It is true that "of making many books there is no end." But we modern writers who write in the Hebrew language keep trying to make up for lost time.

What Do You Think?

All the children who had Bialik as a teacher or a friend loved him very much. On his birthday children would come to his house in Tel Aviv and bring him flowers and small gifts. What kind of a man do you think he was? Do children in the United States do such things? Is there anyone (not a relative) to whom you would bring flowers or a small gift if that was your custom?

Something for You to Do

Look in your school library for pictures of Bialik, for books or poems that he wrote.

Some people say that he introduced the idea of Oneg Shabbat. Pretend to write a letter to him, describing the Oneg Shabbat in your temple. Illustrate it and put it on the bulletin board. Ask your teacher to show the class the filmstrip on Bialik.

You Will Enjoy Reading

"The City of Slaughter," in *The Story of the Jew*, by LEVINGER and GERSH, Behrman House, Inc., p. 180.

Builders of the Jewish People, Vol. II of the History Through Literature Series, by MARTHA MARENOF, Dot Publications (Private), pp. 226-233.

Giants on the Earth, by DEBORAH PESSIN, Behrman House, Inc., pp. 124-133.

And It Came to Pass, by DEBORAH PESSIN, Stories Retold by Bialik, Hebrew Publishing Co.

Some More Facts About Chaim Nahman Bialik

Chaim Nahman Bialik has been called the greatest Hebrew writer since the days of the Bible. Some think him the greatest poet in a thousand years. Many books have been written about his life, his works, his family, and his influence on Jews and non-Jews alike. Everything about his history is important to people who are interested in Jewish life and literature.

In his poetry he wrote about what he saw in the small villages of Eastern Europe, the sad years of childhood and his memories of poverty and pogroms. His desire for knowledge of the world beyond that of his childhood brought him at last, to Palestine, where he felt he could become one of a "first generation of free men."

Bialik tried his hand at being a businessman, but when he realized he was writing poems most of the time, poems about people, their sadness and their hopes, he became a teacher. He wrote and published textbooks for his students. This allowed him time to write of the things which were closest to him.

He wrote in Hebrew and Yiddish and translated his own and other writers' works from one language to another, so that the

Jewish people would be able to read famous books in a language they understood.

Children loved him and loved to listen to his stories. His house in Tel Aviv has become a museum, and people from everywhere come to see it and to pay their respects to his work and his memory.

When he died in 1934, at the age of 61, he was mourned all over the world.

20

LOUIS DEMBITZ BRANDEIS
To Be a Better Jew
Is to Be a Better American

IT IS a tough job to be legal assistant to Louis Brandeis. I
—my name is Jim Allen—ought to know. It's my job. Mr.
Brandeis hired me right after I had graduated from Harvard
Law School. I look up points of law in the library for the boss.
I also run all kinds of errands. He uses me for a sounding
board when his wife Alice isn't around.

Mr. Brandeis doesn't like modern ways of doing things. He
is a very great lawyer and a rich man, but he answers all his
mail with pen and ink. He doesn't want to have his office
cluttered up with secretaries and mechanical equipment. He
expects me to look up the facts and to do the leg work. He
just wants to think and talk and write.

Mr. Brandeis certainly is a very bright man. But one of the

things that makes my work so hard is the way he gets himself, personally, into other people's problems. For example, look at what happened during the garment workers' strike in New York. My boss was called in to help settle the strike. Now, Mr. Brandeis is a Jew. He's not what some Jews might call a very Jewish Jew, but he's a Jew for all that. Almost all of the workers and the owners in the New York garment industry are Jews too.

Well, it was very hot in New York that July. It was made even hotter for us by the tempers of the ten workers and the ten employers packed in the conference room along with their official representatives, their secretaries, Mr. Brandeis and me. Everyone had taken off his coat except my boss. With his wavy hair, cool blue eyes and neat linen jacket, he was every inch the Southern gentleman and Harvard graduate.

Things began fairly well. "Gentlemen," Mr. Brandeis said, "we have come together in a matter which we must all realize is very serious. For the good of workers, owners and consumers, we must settle this strike. But more important, we must work out plans which will help prevent strikes in future years."

One of the employers jumped to his feet. "It's impossible to deal with these workers," he shouted. "They want too much. They want to run our businesses for us. They should be grateful that we give them *jobs*! Where would such greenhorns get jobs to earn their bread, if we did not try to keep our factories open?"

That lit the fuse. One of the workers, a small, pale man with wild hair and burning eyes leaped up on a table. In a

thick Yiddish accent he shouted: "Shame on you! Is this
the way for a Jew to talk? Remember these words:

> The Lord will enter into judgment
> With the elders of His people, and the princes thereof:
> 'It is you that have eaten up the vineyard;
> The spoil of the poor is in your houses;
> What do you mean by crushing My people,
> And grinding the face of the poor?'
> Says the Lord, the God of hosts.

That threw the whole room into an uproar. Mr. Brandeis
banged his gavel for order. Everyone quieted down. He spoke
calmly to the excited worker. "Those words have a Biblical
flavor," he said. "What is the source of your quotation?"

"It's from the Bible, all right," the worker replied, as he
jumped down from the table. "That's what the prophet
Isaiah said to the rich Jews of his time. In God's name, I ask
the same question of these Jews who make us sweat for a
living. They expect us to be thankful for a few crumbs. We
labor long hours under inhuman conditions while they make
fortunes."

It seemed to be an impossible situation, but after many
days of hard work and much soothing of over-heated tempers,
Mr. Brandeis managed to bring the workers and the owners
together. An agreement was reached which established high
union standards for the good of the workers in the garment
industry. The agreement also provided for discussion and a
real attempt at peaceful settlement of difficulties before a
strike could take place.

Because of this experience, Mr. Brandeis had become
deeply interested in the Jews he met, especially the working
men and women. I could see that, after the garment workers'

215

"Shame on you! Is this the way for a Jew to talk?"

affair, my boss had begun to think of himself more and more as a Jew. He took to reading books about Jewish history. Now that I think back upon the events of those days, it seems almost as if he had been preparing himself for something which was to happen about two years later.

One morning I ushered a visitor, Jacob de Haas, into Mr. Brandeis' study. This young man had a very warm manner. "I am the editor of the *Jewish Advocate* in Boston," he explained, speaking with a pleasant British accent. "I have come to ask for some legal advice."

After the legal questions had been answered, Mr. Brandeis asked his visitor about the topics of greatest concern in his Jewish newspaper. Jacob de Haas answered gravely. "Zionism is the great issue of the day, Mr. Brandeis. In my opinion, Zionism is the answer to the future of the Jewish people."

Louis Brandeis was impressed with the earnestness of his guest.

"I'm afraid I don't know very much about Jewish history or the problems of Jewish life today," he said. "Tell me about the Zionist movement. Is it something new? Why don't you stay for lunch so that my two daughters will be able to learn about it too? I'm sorry that Mrs. Brandeis is away on a visit."

Jacob de Haas stayed for lunch and on through the afternoon. Brandeis' two daughters, Elizabeth, who was fourteen and Susan, three years older, listened wide-eyed as their father's guest spoke of the work of the early Jewish pioneers in Palestine. "The love of Zion is as old as our people," he said, "but the Zionist movement of today is quite new. The first Zionist Congress was held just about when you were born,

Elizabeth, under the leadership of a great man named Theodor Herzl. It is our purpose to secure a homeland for our people in Palestine."

Susan asked: "Does that mean that all the Jews will go to live there? Will we have to leave our homes, Mr. de Haas?"

"No, Susan," he smiled. "The Jewish homeland will be for those Jews who need homes, and for those who choose to live there instead of anywhere else. But all of us will be better able to live as Jews if our plan succeeds. There will be a Jewish community living in the old land, speaking the Hebrew language as we speak English. There will be many things we shall be able to learn from them."

That night Louis Brandeis wrote a letter to his brother in Louisville. "I had by chance," he wrote, "one of the original Zionists for lunch yesterday. Susan and Elizabeth agree that he told a more exciting story than the yarns of our friend Captain Baker, the old sailor. I am going to become a Zionist."

Louis Dembitz Brandeis did become a loyal Zionist. As with everything else that he did, he threw himself into these new tasks with all his heart and energy. He worked very hard to raise money for the cause. Whenever he could spare time from his work, he spoke at Jewish meetings, trying to interest other people in Zionism.

Then World War One broke out in Europe. The world center of the Zionist movement moved to the United States. A special Committee for General Zionist Affairs was formed. The people elected Louis Brandeis chairman.

For a while things went smoothly. Brandeis was busy with the law and with Zionism. Then the President of the United

States, Woodrow Wilson, stunned the entire country with one single act. Without telling anyone, the President appointed Louis Dembitz Brandeis to the Supreme Court! It was the very first time in American history that a Jew had been so honored. Newspaper headlines screamed the news: "A great national disaster! Like being hit by a bomb from an unseen Zeppelin!"

"What do you think of the appointment?" my boss asked me. "Will you come with me from Boston to Washington and continue as my legal assistant?"

"It is a very great honor, sir," I answered. "I should like to move to Washington. But please remember that your appointment must first be approved by the Senate of the United States."

"I have not forgotten that," Mr. Brandeis said with a little smile. "Do you think there will be any trouble about it?"

Of course, the boss was joking. He knew perfectly well that there would be plenty of trouble. A committee of the Senate was considering the appointment. If Mr. Brandeis had been an ordinary lawyer or a regular politician, the whole thing would have blown over in a few days. But not in his case. Now it was clear how many people feared and hated him.

Those who opposed the appointment did not say openly that they were against Mr. Brandeis because he had a liberal mind, or because he was a Jew and an active Zionist. Not at all. Hiding their real feelings, they said that he would not make a good judge because he was not a practical man. He had "wild" ideas. He liked to "advertise" himself. He was too selfish. He had a hot temper. He did not have the proper character for a judge of the Supreme Court. Weeks and months went by. Still there was no answer from the committee of the Senate.

The President had made the appointment on January 28. Winter passed, and spring came to New England. Still there was no answer. Tension mounted. The strain began to tell on the Brandeis family.

"Let's go to Bretton Woods for a while," Louis Brandeis said to his wife, Alice. "It will be good for you and the girls. We always enjoy the country in New Hampshire. While we're there, perhaps we can forget the battle in Washington."

They packed and the four of them took the train to Bretton Woods. I stayed on in Washington, waiting for the decision.

It was fortunate that Mr. Brandeis had many friends as well as some enemies. One by one the friendly witnesses stepped forward to tell the truth before the committee. Point by point, they showed that Mr. Brandeis was a man who would make a great and good judge. At last, on May 24, the members of the committee voted on the question. Eight voted against confirming his appointment. Ten voted in favor of it.

The report was sent to the Senate of the United States. There, on June 1, the Senate approved the nomination by a vote of forty-seven to twenty-two. On June 5, President Wilson said: "I am relieved and delighted at the confirmation of Brandeis. I never signed any commission with such satisfaction as I signed his."

I was very happy when I sat in the Senate chamber with the family and friends of the new Justice on his first day as a member of our highest court. There he was, looking very proud in his long, black robe as he faced Chief Justice White.

Holding a Bible in one hand, Mr. Brandeis took the oath to be a fair judge according to the laws and the Constitution of the United States.

I heard one woman sitting near us whisper to her neighbor: "I am about to see a Jew on the Supreme Court of my country for the first time!"

Mr. Brandeis has served on the Court for a long time now. He has done a great deal to advance the cause of justice. He has worked to protect freedom for all of us Americans.

For the Jewish people of the United States, Mr. Brandeis has performed a very special task. After his appointment had been confirmed, some of his friends urged him to give up his interest in Jewish affairs, especially the Zionist movement.

"How can you be a Zionist and still serve as a Justice of the Supreme Court?" one of his friends asked. "Zionism is a political movement which works for Palestine. People will question your loyalty to America if you continue to work for Zionism. I think that you should stop all those Jewish activities and prove to the world that you are one hundred per cent American."

I shall always remember Mr. Brandeis' answer. "I believe," he said thoughtfully, "that to be good Americans, we must be better Jews. To be better Jews, we must become Zionists. Our religion and our history have prepared us to work for the American ideals of democracy and justice. The basic law of America seeks to make real the brotherhood of all men. If we are good Jews, we shall be better Americans. The Zionist movement helps our people stay alive as loyal Jews. That is why it also helps us to be better Americans."

Many American Jews agree with Mr. Brandeis. They have

found help in the example of a man chosen for one of the highest offices in our country who still continued his work for the Jewish people. Many others do not agree with Mr. Brandeis. As for me—Jim Allen—I have my own problems. All these years on the Supreme Court and my boss *still* doesn't like secretaries or office machines! That being the case, I'd better stop writing about Mr. Brandeis and get back to my work!

What Do You Think?

Where is Brandeis University located? Discuss with your parents how this university differs from others in this area. Consider also, was there a need for this university in an area where there are so many others?

Something for You to Do

Learn what these words mean: strike, arbitrate, mediate. Ask your parents to help you compare Louis Brandeis with Arthur Goldberg, Supreme Court Justice. List the ways in which they resemble one another. (This would be an interesting report to share with your classmates.)

You Will Enjoy Reading

The New Jewish History, Book Three, by MAMIE G. GAMORAN, Union of American Hebrew Congregations, pp. 250-261.

The Story of the Jew, by LEVINGER and GERSH, Behrman House, Inc., see index.

Builders of the Jewish People, Vol. II of the History Through Literature Series, by MARTHA MARENOF, Dot Publications (Private), pp. 218-225.

Your Parents Will Enjoy Reading

Giants of Justice, by ALBERT VORSPAN, UAHC, pp. 22-39.

Your Class Will Enjoy Reading

Brandeis by MORTON WISHENGRAD, in The Eternal Light Series, Crown Publishers.

Some More Facts About Louis Dembitz Brandeis

Louis Dembitz Brandeis was born in Louisville, Kentucky, in 1856. He had very little Jewish education. At Harvard Law School, where he was educated, he was known to be an excellent scholar and just a few years after his graduation, he had gained a reputation as a brilliant, honest lawyer. He was not afraid to suggest changes in the practice of law, or to introduce new ideas when he felt they would be for the good of the people. He believed that all men must work for a better world. He was known as "The People's Lawyer."

While arbitrating a strike of Jewish garment workers in New York City, he met many Jews for the first time, and was amazed that his ideas of brotherhood, social justice, and civil liberties were traditionally part of the Jewish way of life. Years later he said: "It is the Jewish tradition and the Jewish law and the Jewish spirit which prepare us for the lessons of life."

He became interested in Zionism and by 1914, was its leading spokesman in America. He helped found the American Jewish Congress, which united Jews in America. When he was appointed Justice of the Supreme Court of the United States in 1916, he had to give up active participation in these groups, but his loyalty and devotion to them remained.

Brandeis University in Waltham, Massachusetts, is named in his honor. There is a settlement in Israel, *Ein Hashofet,* established in his memory. In his will he left a large sum of money for the maintenance of civil liberties and the promotion of workers' education.

He died in 1941.

JUDAH LEON MAGNES

Building the House on the Hill

JUDAH MAGNES tugged at the peak of his cap. He glanced over his shoulder at first base. Hasan, the Arab boy, was pretty far from the bag. "I'd better pitch to Abe Meyer," Magnes thought, "if I throw the ball to first base, our great scientist from France will probably drop it and Hasan will go down to second."

The game was being played in Jerusalem on the Fourth of July. Judah Leon Magnes always organized a baseball game for the Fourth. That was his way of celebrating the holiday which reminded him of his boyhood in Oakland, California. Now that he was President of the Hebrew University in Jerusalem he had little time for games. But today he was pitching for the faculty team. The teachers led by a score of seven to six. It was the first half of the ninth inning. There were two out, but Hasan was on first. He had lined one out to center field for a base hit. Now everything depended on getting young Abe Meyer out. None of the teachers and very few of the students had played much baseball. Since he couldn't count on strong support from the fielders, Dr. Magnes decided to try for a strikeout.

Facing the batter, Judah Magnes wound up for the pitch. He was a tall man with dark hair and a keen, friendly face. Abe watched a straight, fast one whiz by. The catcher, a famous lawyer from England, caught it. Max Schloessinger, scholar of Oriental lore, called out: "Strike one!" Judah Magnes had known Schloessinger ever since they had been students together in Germany. Dr. Magnes had gone to Germany as a young rabbi right after his graduation from the Hebrew Union College. Max Schloessinger could not run very fast any more. That's why he had agreed to umpire.

Judah Magnes tried a curve ball. It was low and outside for ball one. "Why don't you give me something I can hit?" asked the batter.

"I'll try. Let's see how you like this one," answered Judah Magnes. He threw another curve which Abe tipped for a foul ball.

"Strike two," called the umpire. Then Dr. Magnes lost all control of his pitching arm. He threw two balls wide of the plate. It was all the catcher could do to hang on to them. In the confusion Hasan advanced from first to second, then from second to third. Everyone laughed when he clutched the cords of his Arab headdress as he ran. The count on

Abe was now three balls and two strikes. With Hasan in scoring position, everything depended on the next pitch. Judah Magnes wound up. He pitched a slow, high knuckleball. It seemed to float in towards the plate. Abe prepared to wallop the ball. He swung. . . . and missed!

"That's strike three! The game is over," announced Dr. Schloessinger. "The faculty wins by the score of seven to six."

"Thanks for the game, fellows," Dr. Magnes said. He waved goodbye as he left the field and walked down from the campus on Mt. Scopus to his home. His wife, Beatrice, was preparing supper.

"How was the game, Judah?" she asked, smiling, as she untied her apron.

"We did very well, I'm happy to say. It was close, but our teachers managed to win, seven to six. Where is David?"

Mrs. Magnes went to the foot of the stairs. "David," she called, "supper is ready. Please come down." David was a high school student. He had stayed home from the game that afternoon to study. David hoped that someday he might become a teacher at the Hebrew University. His brothers, Jonathan and Baruch, were at school in the United States.

"Hello, Dad," David said, bouncing down the steps two at a time. "Or, should I say *Shalom, Avi*," he added, smiling at his father. "I hear that you old-timers beat the students in today's game."

"That's right, David," his father replied, rubbing his hands. "I can still pitch. . . . a little."

The family gathered round the table and Dr. Magnes gave the blessing. "We thank Thee for the peace of Eretz Yisrael, for the joy of our home, for the food of this table.

226

Boruch atah Adonai. . . ." When he had finished, they sat down to supper.

"Is there much more to do before the meeting of the Board of Governors?" Beatrice Magnes asked her husband.

"There is, indeed," Dr. Magnes said. "Dr. Weizmann is coming for the meeting. And there are so many details to see to. I must try to have everything in good order. But what really bothers me is not the buildings or the grounds. The students are a big help with those things. After all, they built the buildings with their own hands. . . ."

"Yes," David interrupted. "And that's really something to be proud of. I never heard of students in the United States building their school themselves, with their own hands."

Dr. Magnes smiled. "I suppose it has been done before, but not like this. Our students come from all over the world. They are so delighted to be studying in Jerusalem and to have a chance to learn the Hebrew language that they help in every way. But our big problem is peace between the Arab people and the Jews. Ever since the riots last year I have been thinking about how the University can help solve it. The future of the Jewish national home depends on peace. I believe that peace with our neighbors should come before everything else. But not everyone on the Board agrees with me. I am sure there will be a quarrel at the meeting."

"There is one thing I am sure of," Mrs. Magnes said, "you will defend what you think is right, no matter what happens. That's what you did in New York when you were a rabbi. That is what you will do here as President of the University."

"I hope so," Dr. Magnes replied. "But it won't be easy, Bea. There have been fights in the streets. Many of our people have strong feelings about all this. They have suffered in other lands because they were helpless. Now they want to be sure that they are in control of what happens here. I can understand this feeling. But I do not want war with the Arab world. The University must be a center for peace between Jews and Arabs."

As usual, Dr. Magnes got up very early the next morning. The sun was still low in the rosy eastern sky as he left the house. Passing the stable, he called: "Come, Teddy!" A small shepherd dog bounded out of the stable. He barked happily and wagged his tail. Followed by his little friend, Dr. Magnes began the climb toward the Hebrew University, the "house on the hill," as he liked to call it. The stone buildings took on the light and color of the morning sun. First they came to a long, low building which housed many animals from every part of the world. Students at the University studied them in their science courses.

The man who took care of the animal house came out, dressed in an immaculate uniform, to greet Dr. Magnes. "Shalom," he said, "how are you this morning? I see you're up early, as usual."

"Shalom, Ben Menachem. I am well, and hope you are the same. You know that there's to be a very important meeting at the University next week. Be sure the animal pens are clean. And please put some more of that fine gravel on the path leading to this building. It will make the walk look much better."

"It shall be done, Dr. Magnes," said Ben Menachem. "But let me ask you a question. Is it really the job of the President of the University to worry about animal pens and gravel walks? Why don't you leave such things to the people in charge of grounds and buildings?"

"You're right, Ben Menachem, but I can't help being interested in everything that happens at the University. Do you know that I helped plan this house of learning long before there was even one faculty member or student?" He laughed. "I guess I'm like Teddy, here. He's an old dog. He does what he's used to doing very well, but he doesn't learn new tricks. I just can't seem to learn to leave the Hebrew University for someone else to take care of. Well, see you tomorrow." Waving his hand to Ben Menachem, Dr. Magnes continued up the path and further along the campus with Teddy at his heels.

They passed teachers and students. Dr. Magnes greeted them by name. Soon they reached the administration building, a tall, solid structure of grey stone. In front of the building, in a large oval-shaped flower garden, blue, yellow, and reddish blossoms blended their colors in the early morning sunlight. Ehud, the gardener, was sprinkling the flowers with precious water.

Dr. Magnes bent over the edge of the flower beds and picked up a scrap of paper. "Ehud, come over here, please," called Dr. Magnes. Ehud turned off the hose and hurried over.

"*Boker tov*, Dr. Magnes," he said. "Is something wrong?"

"A good morning to you, too, Ehud," Dr. Magnes replied. "Yes, there is something wrong." Opening his hand, he showed Ehud the scrap of paper. "I found this here in the flowers, Ehud. Some careless person, perhaps one of the boys or girls, dropped it. Now, look around. There is more litter in the flower beds and on the paths. I want it all cleaned up. We want our Hebrew University to be a beautiful spot as well as a great center for study."

Ehud nodded in agreement and went back to work. Dr. Magnes moved on with Teddy. He was familiar with every stick and stone of the place. Every day he had a long talk with at least one of the teachers. He knew what each one was studying and teaching. He knew the people who worked for the University. They lived in apartments which Dr. Magnes had had built on the grounds of the campus. He knew the students by name. Apart from his wife and their three sons, the Hebrew University was the most important thing in life for Judah Leon Magnes.

Important visitors from all over the world began to arrive in Jerusalem. They were the members of the Board of Governors. The new school term would start in November. Now, during the summer, plans had to be made for the next year. Professor Saul Adler came from England. Professor Israel Kliger arrived from the United States. Dr. Chaim Weizmann, head of the World Zionist Organization, came from London, as did Dr. Nahum Sokolow, Zionist leader and friend of Weizmann. Some members of the Board lived in Palestine, including the great Hebrew poet, Chaim Nachman Bialik.

On the day of the meeting, Beatrice Magnes insisted that, for once, her husband give up his habit of getting up at dawn. "I want you to have plenty of rest and time for a good breakfast. You will need all your strength for the meeting." Judah Magnes knew his wife was right. There would be plenty of argument about the ideas he was going to present in his report to the Board.

"I feel the way I did in New York before preaching a sermon," he told his wife at breakfast. "No one knows the University as well as I do, and no one on the Board knows Palestine better than I. It is easy to decide what we should be doing in Jerusalem from Warsaw or London or New York. But here—in the midst of the struggle—it is not so simple.

"Well, it is time for me to go. Keep Teddy in today. I don't think some of our Board members would like having him at the meeting." Judah Magnes kissed his wife, patted her shoulder, and set off for the University. As he passed the stable he heard Teddy whimpering sadly behind the closed door.

The small room was crowded when Dr. Weizmann called the meeting to order. He asked for a report from the President of the University. Judah Magnes stood behind the table facing the Board of Governors. *"B'ruchim habaim,"* he began, "blessed are you who have come to help build this center of learning in Eretz Yisrael."

First Dr. Magnes told them everything that had been done during the past year. He told them how many students there were, what countries they came from, and how many books had been added to the library. He introduced the members of the faculty. He described the building work of the students.

"Now, my friends," he continued, "there are two major points I want to make about the future of our University. First, I realize that the study of science is important. We do need to know everything possible about the soil and rainfall of this land. We need to train men who can build bridges and invent machines. We need experts in chemistry and other sciences. But even more than that, we need young men and

231

women who know our history as Jews, people who have studied the Bible and the other great books of Judaism. That is why I say that the study of languages, history, religion, and art is even more important than the study of science."

A murmur arose in the room. Men began to whisper to one another. It was plain that many of the Board members did not agree.

Chaim Weizmann banged his gavel to restore order. "Gentlemen," he spoke loudly, "please be quiet. You know that I am a chemist. I do not agree with this idea of Dr. Magnes about what is most important for us to teach here. But we must listen courteously until he has finished his report. Then you may accept his report or not, as you wish." The room was quiet as Dr. Magnes went on.

"I knew that some of you would not agree with me," he said, "but what I have to say next will be even harder for you to accept. The Jewish community in Palestine is a tiny island in a big Arab sea. The Arabs are our neighbors. I know that they are not always good neighbors, but we have to live with them. That is one reason we have Arab students here in our University. That is also why we have a Department of Arabic Studies. There are two peoples in Palestine. There are three religions here. We must face this problem. We must answer it as Jews. We are men of peace. Here in the Holy Land we should have no enemies, only neighbors and brothers. We must work to make the Hebrew University a center for peace between Arabs and Jews."

Once more the room became noisy as many Board members voiced their disagreement with the President.

Dr. Magnes held up his hand. "One moment more, my

friends, and I shall finish my report to you." He waited for silence. Then, clenching his fist, he said quietly, "I am not ready to try to win justice for the Jews through injustice for the Arabs. I believe in a community where Jews and Arabs will live together with equal rights in peace. If I am not for a Jewish State, it is only for the reason I have stated: I do not want war with the Arab world. Let us make our University a bond of peace between Arabs and Jews."

Dr. Magnes had finished his report. By now the room was crackling with excitement and noise. Some applauded the report. Others shouted: "No! No! We have heard enough about Arabs. The Jewish State and the Hebrew University should be only for Jews!"

Nahum Sokolow jumped to his feet. "Mr. Chairman," he shouted, "I want the floor! I want to speak!" Over and over again, Dr. Weizmann called for order. Gradually the noise died down. Nahum Sokolow went on: "We have heard the report of the President of the University. There is much in it with which we all agree. There is much with which we do not agree. You know that as a friend and close worker with Chaim Weizmann, I understand the need for the final goal of a Jewish State. I also know that, to support that State, we shall need men of science to build up the land. But I say to you that now is *not* the time for us to seek our final goal. Let us accept this report and go along for the present with the ideas of Dr. Magnes, who has worked so hard for the University. When the time comes to found the Jewish State, we shall do it. Let us pray that it may be done in peace. But whether peace or war prevails, we will have a Jewish State some day.

The majority voted to accept the President's report. That evening, as they sat watching the lights of the city go on, one by one, Judah Magnes told Beatrice what had happened at the meeting.

"It is only a victory for today," he said. "Most of the Board members have no hope for Jewish-Arab unity. They want to force the creation of a Jewish State. But, much as I love the hills and valleys and the peoples of this land, if we can't learn how to live together in peace, I am afraid of what the future may bring."

"I know, Judah," Beatrice said quietly. "But I sometimes think you are a dreamer. Our people have suffered so much in other lands. They cannot always be reasonable. And it is just as hard to deal with the Arab leaders. They, too, have their grudge and anger. Things will probably get worse in Palestine before they get better."

"Perhaps you are right," Judah answered. "But what I believe was all said long ago. Remember? 'Zion shall be redeemed through justice,' It is the only way." And the lights of the city seemed to shine brighter, as if to answer him.

What Do You Think?

What was Magnes' position before he became President of the Hebrew University? In which position could he serve the Jewish people better? Why do you think so?

Something for You to Do

Find pictures of the Hebrew University in Jerusalem, the Hebrew Union College in Jerusalem, and the Technion in Haifa. What is studied in each one? Who is the president of each college? Can you find pictures of these people?

You Will Enjoy Reading

A *History of the Jews in the United States,* by LEE J. LEVIN-GER, Union of American Hebrew Congregations, see index for Hebrew University and Judah L. Magnes.

Reform Judaism in the Making, by SYLVAN D. SCHWARTZ-MAN, UAHC, pp. 132 and 182.

The Junior Jewish Encyclopedia, ed. by NAOMI BEN-ASHER and HAYIM LEAF, Shengold Publishers, Inc., see Hebrew University; also Judah L. Magnes.

Some More Facts About Judah Leon Magnes

Judah Leon Magnes was born in San Francisco, California, in 1877. He was ordained at the Hebrew Union College and served as rabbi to several congregations in New York. During this early part of his career in New York, he realized that there were many small Jewish organizations all working separately for the same goals—food, shelter, clothing, medical supplies, and relocation for needy Jews. He persuaded the leaders of these groups to join together in order to make their efforts more effective. Thus the *Kehilla* of New York was formed. It guided and advised congregations, organizations, and even local governments in Jewish affairs. The example of the Kehilla was copied in other cities. The Federations of today are based on Dr. Magnes' idea of the Kehilla.

He was a great American Zionist, and one of his most cherished dreams was a university in Palestine. He moved to Jerusalem with his family, to help establish the University. He was its first president and held that position for twenty-five years.

His belief that Jews and Arabs could live in peace together in Palestine was not shared by many people and at times made him very unpopular, but he never gave up the hope that some day, "brothers would live together in peace."

He died in 1947.

22

ALBERT EINSTEIN
The Most Famous Scientist of our Time

IN his youth, Albert Einstein had a great deal of trouble with school work in his home town in Germany. "Albert," his history teacher would ask him, "why can't you remember the dates of the wars fought by the Romans? The other boys remember. I don't believe you study your lessons."

Albert's large, dark eyes were very serious. "Yes, Herr Professor, I *did* study the lesson. But I hate to memorize dates. I just can't seem to remember them. There are so many other things I would rather do."

"What would you rather do?" his teacher asked.

"Well," Albert ran his fingers through his thick hair, "in geometry class I have already read the whole book. That really interests me. I want to find out things about the world, what makes it work."

"But Albert," his teacher said sternly, "if you only study one subject, you will never amount to anything. You are a poor student in history, and in languages, too. You had better stop dreaming and get down to work."

This, of course, made Albert feel very sad. At home he would go out to the garden and sit alone, brooding about how poorly he seemed to fit into the orderly, day-to-day life which most boys seemed to find so natural and so easy.

"Poor boy," his father said to Albert's mother. "His little sister Maja is already brighter than Albert. He was so slow in learning how to speak. And now he does so badly at school. I wish I could help him, but I just don't know how."

But Albert did poorly at school because the German schools were run like military academies. The children were drilled like little soldiers and Albert hated it. He could not bring himself to study a lesson just to be able to repeat what he had read in class, like a parrot.

Later on, his parents and Maja moved to Italy but Albert remained in Germany. He became ill and, to his joy, he was dropped from school, which enabled him to join his family. He liked Italy much better than Germany. The air was sunny and warm. The people were happy and friendly. They seemed much freer than the people of Germany. They sang gay songs as they went about their work and the air was full of laughter. Albert loved to play Italian songs on his violin. He wandered about the bright countryside, listening to the songs, thinking his thoughts.

When the time came to go back to school, Albert asked his father to let him study in Zurich in Switzerland.

"Our business isn't going well," his father told him. "But I know how much this means to you. I can send you to Zurich and pay the tuition for the first term but after that, Albert, I'm afraid you will have to support yourself."

Grateful for his father's help. Albert said goodbye to the family and entered school in Zurich. He found the people there, as in Italy, freer and happier than in Germany. Albert was still not the best student in his class, except in mathematics and physics, but he did better than before. He managed to graduate. It was then that Albert decided to become a citizen of Switzerland.

As an older student and after his graduation, Albert Einstein was barely able to make a living as a teacher. But a friend from the University told him that there was an opening for a clerk in the government Patent Office in the city of Bern. "Why don't you try for it, Albert?" his friend asked.

"What does a clerk have to do?" Albert wondered. "I am a teacher. What do I know about patents?"

"But that's just it, Albert," his friend insisted. "You know a lot about mathematics and physics. The Patent Office deals with new inventions. Your job would be to study each new invention and write a short paper, telling the basic facts about it. Then the government officials would decide whether or not to grant the inventor a patent."

"I suppose there would be no harm in trying for the job," Albert said. "I am a Swiss citizen, and I do have my degree from Zurich."

Albert took a long and very difficult written examination.

After waiting for weeks, he received a letter which read: "You have been appointed clerk to the government Patent Office in Bern. You are to report for work there on Monday morning."

He was happy in his new job. He called his work a "shoemaker's job" because he did the same kind of task day after day. For the first time in his life, however, he earned a fairly good living. Each month he was paid promptly. His knowledge of science grew and he found it easy to understand and describe the inventions that were brought to him.

Sometimes there were no inventions to describe. Then Albert turned to his own work, filling page after page with penciled notes of his own ideas. "What is electricity?" he wrote. Then Albert tried to explain it in mathematical terms. "Why do tacks or nails stick to a magnet?" Albert looked for a real answer. "Why does the moon go around the earth instead of spinning off to the sun?" Albert wrote papers about problems like these. Four of them were published in a magazine of science.

When he had finished his fifth scientific paper, Albert put it in the pocket of his shabby coat and set off to see the editor of the magazine. People smiled as they saw him in the streets of Bern. His hair was always tousled and a little too long. There was a faraway look in his deep eyes. He often forgot to wear socks, and spent very little time taking care of his clothes.

At the magazine office, Albert stood before the editor's desk. He took the paper from his pocket. "I have something here for your next issue," he said.

"That's very good of you, Dr. Einstein," the editor replied, "but our next issue is pretty full already."

"This paper isn't very long," Einstein said. "I think it may interest quite a few people."

The editor agreed to publish the paper, not knowing that it was to be one of the most important contributions ever made towards a new understanding of the world. It was Einstein's idea of relativity.

Many leaders of the scientific world were deeply impressed by Dr. Einstein's work. It was no longer necessary for him to go about the tasks of his "shoemaker's job" at the Patent Office. He was offered several positions as professor at great universities. He finally decided to go to Prague, which was then a part of the Austro-Hungarian Empire.

Life in Prague was very different from Bern. Soon after his arrival, Einstein was called to the office of the Rector, the man in charge of the university. He had a pointed waxed moustache and close-cropped hair and spoke like a military officer.

"I welcome you to Prague, Dr. Einstein," he said in a rather sharp voice. "It is also my duty to tell you that you you must state your religion on our official form. All professors in the Empire must state their religious belief."

Dr. Einstein thought about this for a moment. Then he said: "As you may know, my parents are Jewish. I am not sure about religious beliefs. As a scientist I sometimes think. . . ."

The Rector interrupted the new professor. "Dr. Einstein, I did not ask you about your scientific opinions. What is your religion?"

"Very well, then," he answered, "I register myself as a Jew. To me, God is the source of order and harmony in the whole universe. And though I may not be a religious man, I am certainly not ashamed of my parents and my people."

"That will be sufficient," the Rector said. "Christian, Moslem, Jewish. . . . all we want to know is what you *are*. Now, Dr. Einstein, let me inform you that you must purchase a uniform for your formal installation as professor."

"Me, wear a uniform!" Einstein laughed. "I have never done that in my whole life! I even have trouble remembering to wear *socks*."

"Never mind that," the Rector continued. "You must secure the proper uniform. You will wear a feathered hat, a coat with gold braid suitable to your rank, and you will also have a sword."

"If I must, then I must," replied Dr. Einstein, "as long as I only have to wear it once."

After his meeting with the Rector of the University, Albert Einstein went for a walk to think about these peculiar rules. He wandered into the ghetto, the old Jewish section of the city. High in the tower of a building he noticed a huge clock. The clock had Hebrew letters which told the time. "That reminds me of the days when I was a boy and went to Hebrew school," he thought. "I was far from one of the rabbi's best students. Even today, I am not the kind of Jew who observes religious customs. But I am indeed a Jew. Since the Rector insisted that I put down something, I'm glad I registered as Jewish."

Near the hall with the clock, he discovered the old synagogue. It was built like a fort, with thick walls and tiny, slit-like windows. Many times the Jews of Prague had gathered there to escape the mobs raiding their homes.

Nearby, he found the ancient Jewish cemetery. He wandered about, reading the Hebrew inscriptions on the tombstones. Many of the letters were almost erased by the years of wind, rain and snow.

It was in Prague that Einstein first met Jews who were members of the Zionist movement. Some of them became his friends. He went to Zionist meetings in the homes of his Jewish friends. Einstein seldom spoke at these meetings. He sat quietly, puffing away at his pipe, lost in his own thoughts.

He became so well known for his work that a few years later he was invited to move to Berlin, the capital of Germany. "Not long ago," he told his friends, "I had trouble finding even one job in Switzerland. Now I am asked to Berlin to serve in three positions. I am to be a member of the Prussian Academy of Sciences, a professor at the University of Berlin, and Director of the Kaiser Wilhelm Institute for special research in physics. I was not happy in Germany when I was a boy. Perhaps it will be different now that I can work at what interests me."

At the beginning, Einstein was happy in Berlin. He made many friends, among them Fritz Haber, a very well-known chemist. But in 1914, the German armies invaded Belgium and the First World War began.

Fritz Haber was a patriotic German. He became very excited about the war. Since he wanted the Germans to win, he helped them by using his scientific knowledge to make new kinds of explosives and artificial fertilizers. Einstein thought that Germany was at least as much at fault as England or France for having started the terrible war. He wanted only peace, and went about his daily tasks in his usual way.

One day Haber asked Einstein to meet him for lunch. The two men ate potatoes and drank cups of bitter artificial coffee. In war-time Germany, things like meat and coffee were hard to find.

Haber leaned across the table and said intently: "Albert, you know I didn't suggest that we meet here to eat because I thought the food would be delicious. I have something important to ask you. The war is going badly for us Germans. Why don't you devote yourself to making an explosive, or something that will help us win?"

Einstein put down his cup. "I know how you feel about it, Fritz," he said slowly. "But I feel differently. I am loyal to mankind, not just to Germany. I am a Swiss citizen. But if I were still a German citizen, I would continue with my studies, just as before. This war is like an eclipse of the sun. Some day it will pass. In clear sunlight, we shall again see that all men are brothers."

Since Haber and Einstein were really friends, they could disagree and still like each other. But many people turned against Albert Einstein because he spoke out for a just and peaceful world. After the war ended with the defeat of Germany, the sunlight which Dr. Einstein had predicted would brighten the world was often darkened. The German people suffered. In growing numbers they turned to the false leadership of Adolf Hitler, the cruel enemy of the Jews and of all civilized men. Hitler blamed the Jews for the troubles of Germany. He proposed to destroy them all, take over their property and lead a new Germany to victory over the world. And at first Albert Einstein could not believe that such evil could win the loyalty of the educated, cultured German people.

In 1921 Dr. Einstein visited the United States with Chaim Weizmann, the leader of the Zionist movement. They made the trip to help raise money for land in Palestine and to start the Hebrew University in Jerusalem. Even far across the sea, vast numbers of people had heard of Albert Einstein, the world-famous scientist. At Princeton he was introduced by the President of the University as "the new Columbus of science, voyaging through the strange seas of thought alone."

Through his work as a scientist, Albert Einstein had brought praise and fame to Germany from all over the world. People thought of him as a German scientist. But now most of the German people had begun to think with their blood instead of with their minds. The ugliness of anti-Semitism poisoned the air of Germany. It was very fortunate for Einstein and his wife, Elsa, that he was already well known in the United States when Hitler came to power in Germany in 1933. A reward of five thousand dollars had actually been offered by Hitler's Nazis for the arrest of Germany's most famous scientist! But Dr. Abraham Flexner of the Princeton Institute for Advanced Study had invited Dr. Einstein to join his staff. The Einsteins left their home and everything they had worked so hard to achieve in Germany, and escaped to America.

Once more, Albert Einstein began his life's work in a new place. The family moved into a tidy house on Mercer Street in Princeton, New Jersey. The neighbors and townspeople soon became accustomed to seeing the man with the windblown hair, now grey, and the faraway look in his dark eyes. He always wore an old turtle-neck sweater; as always, his trousers were baggy, and he often forgot to wear socks, even though Elsa scolded him. People found him a very friendly man who always had a kind word for neighbors, passing workmen, and, especially, little children.

When they arrived in Princeton, Dr. Flexner asked Einstein what he would need to be comfortable. "I have everything I need," Einstein answered. "We were lucky enough to get some of our furniture out of Germany. As for my work, you know that all I need is a pencil and paper."

"I was talking about money, Dr. Einstein," Flexner explained. "We must settle on the amount of salary the Institute will pay you. If not, how will you buy food and the things you will need for your household?"

"Now I see what you mean," Dr. Einstein nodded his head wisely. "Of course, people need money. Now, let me see. . . ." he ran his hand through his hair, "I read in the paper that it is very expensive to live here. I hate to make it difficult for you, but I'm afraid it will cost us three or maybe even four thousand dollars a year to live here."

Dr. Flexner smiled. "Dr. Einstein," he said, "I see that you are not the business brains of the family. Perhaps if you will permit me to discuss this matter with Mrs. Einstein, we can arrive at a proper amount."

"Yes, by all means," Einstein laughed, "I have no head for figures . . . at least not when it comes to money." Dr. Flexner discussed the problem with Mrs. Einstein and they decided upon a salary several times that which Dr. Einstein had suggested.

The years at Princeton passed peacefully. Albert Einstein was growing old. He did not play the violin as often now. He was not allowed to smoke his pipe. But faithfully, day after day, he went on with his work.

245

The world outside the university town was far from peaceful. After they had built the world's greatest, most terrifying military machine, the German Nazis invaded the countries of their neighbors. The Second World War spread almost throughout the entire world. After Japan, Germany's ally, bombed the American base at Pearl Harbor, the United States declared war on Germany. This was at the end of 1941. Professor Einstein had always loved and worked for peace. But now he realized that if the Nazis won the war, all free men would become their slaves.

One day a group of very distinguished scientists visited Dr. Einstein in Princeton. One of them, Leo Szilard, had known him during his years in Berlin. "Dr. Einstein," Leo Szilard said, "let me introduce a colleague, Dr. Enrico Fermi from Italy. You are already acquainted with the third member of our committee, Professor Wigner of Princeton."

Dr. Einstein greeted the visitors and led the men into his book-lined study.

Leo Szilard spoke: "Let me come to the point quickly, Dr. Einstein. We have come to you on an absolutely secret and most urgent mission. Your discovery of relativity has had an unexpected effect. It is now possible to release and control the atomic energy locked in uranium ore. This means that someone, *someone* will soon develop a bomb more powerful than any ever made before. We know that the Nazi scientists are working on this. We also know that recently there have been large-scale imports of uranium ore into Germany."

"But, Dr. Szilard," Albert Einstein interrupted him, "you know that my work was never meant to be of practical use. It is theoretical. I am not interested in explosives. I have

"We have come to you on an absolutely secret and most urgent mission."

devoted my life to trying to find out the nature of the universe."

"Yes, we know that," said Leo Szilard. "But in spite of your love of peace, your discoveries have made the production of an atomic bomb possible. You are the most famous scientist in the United States. We have come to ask that you write to President Franklin D. Roosevelt and urge him to set up a tremendous scientific project to carry on this work. He will listen to you, and to *you alone*. If we start at once, and devote all our energies to it, we shall release and control atomic energy before Germany does. We shall be able to build a weapon so powerful that we can end the war."

Einstein sat lost in thought. His visitors were silent as they waited for his decision. "All my life," he thought, "I have struggled and sacrificed for peace. But now. . . . I know from my own experience that the Nazis are more like mad beasts than men. It is true that the future of all free men depends on stopping them before it is too late."

Silently, Einstein reached for pen and paper. While the other scientists waited, he wrote to the President of the United States about the atom bomb and the danger that the Nazis might be able to make it first. The letter was delivered to President Roosevelt by a trusted messenger. The President acted upon the matter at once, and the project was under way.

The secrets of nature which Albert Einstein had come to understand were released and the atomic age had begun. Dr. Einstein lived to see the end of the war and the beginning of a new age he had done so much to make possible.

What Do You Think?

Dr. Einstein received the Nobel Prize. For what reason is

248

this prize given? What is the prize? For what did Dr. Einstein receive this prize? Should he have received this honor?

Something for You to Do

List all the statements Albert Einstein made about his religious ideas.

List all the activities in which he participated that identify him with *Klal Yisrael*.

Ask your teacher to show your class the filmstrip, *Einstein,* Jewish Education Committee of New York.

You Will Enjoy Reading

"Discoverer of Universes" (Albert Einstein), in *American Jewish Heroes*, by Rose G. Lurie, Union of American Hebrew Congregations, New York, 1960.

Your Parents Will Enjoy Reading

Giants of Justice, by ALBERT VORSPAN, Union of American Hebrew Congregations, pp. 76-94.

(If they make up a list like yours above, you can compare your findings.)

Some More Facts About Albert Einstein

Albert Einstein was born in Ulm, Germany, in 1879. He had always been a peaceful man and a pacifist until World War II, when the Nazis in Germany drove him to seek another home. Americans were proud to welcome him to the United States. He joined the staff of the Princeton Institute for Advanced Studies, where, with his family, he spent the last years of his life.

Einstein believed that "only a life lived for others is a life worth living." He also believed that Judaism was democracy in action, and that social justice is the right of all men; that truth, justice, and liberty for all men must always be important to the Jewish people.

He became an active member of the Zionist organization, and set a splendid example for others who wished to help create a homeland for homeless Jews. Though he was a shy, quiet man

249

who loved music and a life of privacy and contemplation, he lectured throughout the United States to help raise funds for the building of the Hebrew University in Jerusalem.

He is considered one of the greatest scientists who ever lived, and it is felt that his ideas have changed the whole course of human history in many ways. He was loved and respected by men all over the world as a great thinker and one who truly loved his fellow men.

He died in 1955.

23

DAVID BEN GURION
First Prime Minister of the State of Israel

TEN boys sat close together in a circle in an empty shack outside the town of Plonsk in Poland. They had met to form a secret society of young Jews.

"What shall we call our group, David?" Shlomo asked the leader, a short stocky boy named David Green.

David answered very seriously. "Let's call ourselves the Ezra Society. Remember Ezra in the Bible? He went back to the land of Israel from Babylon to help rebuild the Hebrew nation. Like Ezra we shall go to Palestine to help free the Jewish people. Now," David went on, "each member of the Ezra Society must swear a solemn oath. Repeat these words after me."

251

David spoke carefully and slowly. The other boys repeated after him: "I do solemnly swear . . . that from now on . . . as long as I live . . . I shall speak only Hebrew!"

"But, David," Shlomo objected, "how can we keep our promise? Some of the boys don't know how to speak Hebrew. Why, your last name is Green. That's not Hebrew. Do you mean that none of us could ever even say your name?"

David explained. "The oath really means that we all promise to study Hebrew and to speak Hebrew just as much as possible. As for my name, I plan to go to Eretz Yisrael. Some day I shall change the name Green to a Hebrew name. I shall keep my first name, David. My full name will be David Ben Gurion."

It so happened that Shlomo Zemach went to Eretz Yisrael before David Ben Gurion. After his friend had left, David went to Warsaw, the great city near his home town. There he became a leader of the young people in the Jewish community. When his friend Shlomo returned, they worked together to raise money to help the Jews in Palestine.

"There are two things we must work for," David said to Shlomo. "The first is a free Jewish life in Eretz Yisrael. But even that won't do much good if the people there must live as the people do here. Just look around you, Shlomo. The masses of men are very poor. A tiny number of men grow rich, while the rest work just to buy bread. Workers must be taught to organize in unions. Then we can help build a better world for all people."

David soon had a chance to test his ideas in the land of Israel. When Shlomo was to return to Palestine, David decided to go with him. He said goodbye to his parents and set off with his friend. After a long trip over land and across the sea they came to the Jewish town of Petach Tikvah in Palestine. David was very happy to be there. He loved the smell of crops growing in the fields, the sound of braying donkeys along the narrow farm lanes. He tried his hand at all kinds of work. He was a worker in the fields and in the wine cellars where the great vats of wine were stored. He was assistant editor of a newspaper. He worked, spoke at meetings, and traveled through the land. Everywhere he went, he told the young people that to be free they would have to be strong and rely on themselves. He told them that they must work together to build a just society which would belong to the people who really did the work.

In those days Palestine was part of the Turkish Empire. When the First World War came, the Turkish officials told David he would have to leave the country. "You talk too much about Jewish independence. Besides, you have friends in England. England is the enemy of Turkey. You must get out of the country within twenty-four hours or you will spend the rest of the war in prison."

David was not too sad about leaving. No more Jews could hope to enter Palestine during the fighting. Perhaps if he went somewhere else, he could organize a Jewish army that would help defeat the Turks and their allies. So David made his first trip to the United States.

In America, David continued his work for Zionism and for the rights of workers on farms and in factories. One night in New York he went to a party at the home of some friends. He noticed a girl there who appealed to him very much. Her name was Paula Munweiss. She spoke very directly. He found her easy to talk to.

"I see that you and I think the same way about many

253

problems of life today," David said earnestly to Paula. "May I ask you a personal question?"

"Of course," Paula answered, "what is it?"

"Well," David hesitated, "I notice that most of the girls here are all dressed up in the new American styles. Why do you wear a plain black skirt and a white blouse? Not that it isn't becoming to you," he blushed, hoping he hadn't said the wrong thing.

Paula laughed. "That's easy to explain. Today is the birthday of a great woman, Emma Goldman. She always dresses like this. We call this an 'Emma Goldman outfit.' I dress this way on her birthday because she cares about the welfare of workers and farmers, just as you and I do. That explains the black skirt and white blouse."

David Ben Gurion was very surprised, both at Paula's answer and at her frank way of speaking to him. He saw her often after that first night. He took her to Zionist and socialist meetings. Toward the end of the war they were married and went together to Palestine.

Great Britain was now in control of Palestine. There had been a Jewish Legion of soldiers in Palestine which Ben Gurion helped General Allenby to organize when General Allenby captured Jerusalem from the Turks. The British government had issued the Balfour Declaration, promising to help establish "a homeland for the Jewish people in Palestine." These events and the fact that there was peace in the world once more encouraged many Jews to go to Eretz Yisrael. As the country grew, David Ben Gurion kept right on working day and night for his two great ideas. "Jews should be strong and independent," he told the people. "Jews should organize as workers and farmers into a great union and work together to build a just society."

Not long after David and Paula had come to Palestine, Ben Gurion was successful in starting the union of workers and farmers. He called it *Histadrut*, the General Federation of Israel Labor. At an early meeting of the executive board of Histadrut, David Ben Gurion made a very remarkable statement.

"Our union is off to a good start," he said. "There are more people employed, and wages are up. But we have done nothing about those people in the country who are the poorest of all. I mean the Arab workers and farmers. I urge you to open membership in the Histadrut to Arabs as well as Jews."

The response to this surprised even Ben Gurion. It was as if he had tossed a bomb into the room. Loud, angry voices were heard on every side. One man shook his fist at Ben Gurion as he demanded the right to speak.

"You must be out of your mind," the angry man protested. "How far would we get organizing Arab workers so that they could demand higher wages from their Jewish employers? Besides, if we help the Arabs get jobs, there won't be nearly enough work for us Jews. I say your idea is all wrong."

Ben Gurion answered the angry man calmly. "The amount of work available is not like water in a pail. Spill some water out and there is less left in the pail. But with a union like the Histadrut, if there aren't enough jobs, I say we can create them. Let's build our own factories, run our own stores and bus lines and banks. We ought to have our own schools, hospitals and theaters, too. That's what I mean by a union, a real progressive force at the heart of the whole community. As for the Arabs, our whole tradition teaches us to care about the stranger and to help all men who are in need. Let's not be afraid. As I've told you before, if we build with courage and justice, we shall win out."

After a long heated discussion the board voted to support Ben Gurion. Arab workers began to join the Histadrut. Then Ben Gurion started a political party called the Mapai. The Mapai party was organized to carry out the same ideas in political life which the Histadrut wanted for those who worked in farm settlements and factories. Ben Gurion was head of the party as well as the union.

The Jews in Palestine were struggling slowly toward national independence. Great Britain was still in control of the country. By now, the Jews had so many local agencies of public affairs that they formed the Jewish Agency to represent all the Jews of Palestine. Ben Gurion was soon elected chairman of the Jewish Agency.

The British government had a great deal of trouble in Palestine. There were riots of Arabs against Jews. It began to seem as though the two peoples could never live together in peace. The British sent many commissions to study the situation. One of these issued the Peel Report, suggesting that Palestine be divided (partitioned) between the Arabs and the Jews.

Most of the leading Zionists in the world were against this partition. Ben Gurion spoke in the World Zionist Congress in favor of dividing the land because this would mean the establishment of an independent Jewish state. He told the people: "The best possible government by another power, as in the case of Britain, can never compare to having a government of our own. I tell you that this is the beginning of the redemption for which we have waited two thousand years."

Before things could be settled one way or the other, the Second World War began. Now the Jews of Europe were being tortured and killed by the Nazis. Those who managed to escape demanded the right to come to Eretz Yisrael. But the British were afraid to stir up Arab unrest during a time of war. They issued a White Paper which limited Jewish immigration to Palestine to only fifteen thousand a year for five years and promised to make Palestine an independent Arab state.

Jewish leaders in Palestine and throughout the world were very disappointed and angry. "What shall we do now?" the people asked. "The Nazi Germans are our real enemies. They are at war against the British. But the British, who have been our friends, have betrayed their promise to us. Shall we fight the war, or shall we fight the White Paper?"

Ben Gurion had an answer. He said: "We will fight the White Paper as if there were no war, and the war as if there were no White Paper." That is just what the Jews did. They fought the White Paper by landing shiploads of illegal immigrants on the shores of Eretz Yisrael under cover of night. They fought the war by organizing a strong Jewish army, the Haganah, which helped drive the Nazis out of North Africa.

When the war ended, the British announced they would give up control of Palestine on May 14, 1948. The United Nations had already voted to divide Palestine into two separate, independent states, one Arab and one Jewish. They had set out the boundaries for these states carefully.

A meeting of representatives of all the Jews in Eretz Yisrael was called for four o'clock in the afternoon of May 14. It was held in the Municipal Museum of the city of Tel Aviv. David Ben Gurion called the meeting to order and rose to speak. He stood directly beneath a portrait of Theodor Herzl who had dreamed of a new Jewish State over half a century before.

Heavier now than in his youth, with his white hair framing his head, Ben Gurion told his people the greatest news in hundreds of years of Jewish history.

"The Land of Israel was the birthplace of the Jewish people," he began. A few minutes later he concluded his speech by announcing: "I hereby declare this meeting adjourned. The State of Israel has come into being."

But there was very little time to express the wild feeling of joy in the hearts of the people of Israel. Early the next morning an Egyptian plane bombed Tel Aviv. That same morning, the country was invaded by the armies of five neighboring Arab nations. These were soon joined by soldiers from two other Arab states. The Israeli army units went to their positions of defense. With superior numbers and equipment, the Arabs expected an easy victory over the new-born state. David Ben Gurion found himself Prime Minister and Minister of Defense of a nation about to be destroyed before it had really begun to live. Ben Gurion worked day and night, often sleeping on a cot at army headquarters.

For twenty-seven days the fighting went on. On almost every front the Israelis advanced against their enemies. A trucc was declared, but fighting soon broke out again. Once more the Israelis fought bravely. They captured Lydda, Ramle and Nazareth. They made the Negev desert a part of the State of Israel. When the next truce was agreed upon, the Israelis found, strangely enough, that although they had lost small areas of the original state, they now had more land than before. The Arab invasion had failed completely.

One of Ben Gurion's first official acts as Prime Minister was to inform Chaim Weizmann, who was then in New York, that he had been chosen to be the first President of Israel. Crowds gathered outside the Waldorf Astoria Hotel where Dr. Weizmann was staying. A great cheer went up from the people in the streets when they saw the blue and white flag with the Star of David, the flag of Israel, raised in front of the hotel in the heart of New York City. It was a tribute to the new President of Israel.

Later on, the coffin of Theodor Herzl was flown to Israel. The founder of the modern Zionist movement was buried in a special tomb on the soil of Israel.

The beautiful Hebrew University, of which Judah Leon Magnes had been President, could no longer be used. It was in a zone of Jerusalem which had come under Arab control. Ben Gurion comforted the people about the loss of the University. "The campus may be lost, but the University lives. We shall continue the work of learning in temporary buildings. Soon we shall build a new campus for the University and the Hadassah hospital."

For many years during the most trying times of the new State of Israel, David Ben Gurion served as Prime Minister. He never lost his love for his people, his passion for social justice, or his vast store of youthful energy. People all through the world recognize and respect this stocky man with the tousled fringe of white hair. He is the hero of the rebirth of Israel.

What Do You Think?

What did the Balfour Declaration accomplish? For what purpose was the White Paper issued? Whom did it help, the Arabs or the Jews? What was the suggestion made in the Peel Report?

Something for You to Do

1. Make a wall chart of the Hebrew words in the story: David, Shlomo, Ezra, Eretz Yisrael, Petach Tikvah, Histadrut, Mapai, Haganah.
2. List the achievements of David Ben Gurion. Which are still important?

You Will Enjoy Reading

"Israel," in *New People in an Old Land*, by L. EDELMAN, J. P. Nelson and Sons.

Israel Today, by HARRY ESSRIG and ABRAHAM SEGAL, Union of American Hebrew Congregations.

The Story of the Jew, by LEVINGER and GERSH, Behrman House, Inc., see index.

Discovering Israel, by TOR, Random House.

Some More Facts About David Ben Gurion

David Ben Gurion was born in Plonsk, Poland, in 1886. He studied law at the University of Constantinople, in Turkey. He came to Palestine in 1906. His early interest in Zionism led to his arrest by the Turkish government, which sentenced him to death for his activities. At the last moment his sentence was changed to that of deportation. He escaped to the United States, but returned to Palestine to fight with honor in the Jewish Legion during World War I. After the war he rose to leadership in the Palestine labor movement.

He has been called the architect of the Jewish State and has served it faithfully in the very difficult years before and after the establishment of the State of Israel. For several years he was not only the Prime Minister, but the Minister of Defense, too. He has always had a remarkable understanding of events as they took place in other parts of the world, and a firm faith in the future of Israel. There are some who think him one of the greatest statesmen and political leaders in the world today.

He is now retired from office in the Israeli government. He lives in a settlement in the Negev. He feels today as he has always felt—that the State of Israel will succeed as long as we all continue to work for it.

UNION GRADED SERIES
Edited by
ALEXANDER M. SCHINDLER, *Director of Education*
UNION OF AMERICAN HEBREW CONGREGATIONS